W9-AXF-282

Imagining la Chica Moderna

Joanne Hershfield

Imagining la Chica Moderna

WOMEN, NATION, AND VISUAL CULTURE

IN MEXICO, 1917–1936

Duke University Press Durham and London 2008

© 2008 Duke University Press
All rights reserved
Printed in the United States of
America on acid-free paper ∞
Designed by C. H. Westmoreland
Typeset in Carter & Cone Galliard
by Keystone Typesetting, Inc.
Library of Congress Cataloging-
in-Publication Data appear on the
last printed page of this book.

For my parents,

SYD & SALLY HERSHFIELD

social- Flapper
cultural- exotic chapter 5
economic - working

Contents

Illustrations

Acknowledgments

I want to acknowledge the people and institutions who have helped me intellectually, emotionally, and technically with this project. First of all, I received generous assistance in the form of time and money through an R. J. Reynolds Research and Leave Fellowship at the University of North Carolina (UNC), Chapel Hill. This fellowship provided me time off from teaching responsibilities as well as a travel grant that allowed me to conduct research in Mexico. I also want to thank the Duke-UNC Institute for Latin American Studies for granting me a number of Title VI Faculty Summer Research Awards that supported summer research in Mexico in 2003 and 2005.

Archivists in Mexico and the United States helped me immensely as I spent many enjoyable days searching through their collections. I especially want to thank the staff of the Benson Latin American Collection at the University of Texas, Austin; the staff of the Biblioteca Miguel Lerdo de Tejada in Mexico City, and the Biblioteca Pública de Guadalajara, Sección de Fondos Especiales, Universidad de Guadalajara. In Mexico, John Mraz, Eli Bartra, Ángel Miquel Patricia Torres San Martín, and Alva Lai Shin offered food, drink, companionship, advice, and research assistance. In the United States, Susan Toomey Frost kindly opened up her wonderful collection of Mexican postcards for my perusal and helped locate the images I needed from her carefully organized archive.

Friends and colleagues who supported me through the research and writing of the book are too numerous to mention, but I want especially to single out Jan Bardsley for her sharp editorial eye and willingness to read through various drafts of the manuscript; Michael and Katy Mullen for providing room, board, and good company in Austin; and Barbara Harris and Jane Burns for taking me under their wings. Many thanks to the staff at Duke University Press who helped guide this project to completion, especially my editor, Valerie Millholland, whose commitment to critical scholarship on Latin American history and culture is greatly appreciated by so many of us. And, finally, but most important, love and thanks to Jim Fink, who provided sustenance in all of its possible manifestations. Without his love, support, encouragement, and technological expertise, this manuscript might have taken another five years.

Imagining la Chica Moderna

modern woman

1. "What's changed between yesterday and today," *Ilustrado*,
3 October 1929, unpaginated.

Introduction

History decomposes into images, not stories.
WALTER BENJAMIN, *The Arcades Project*, 476

The cartoon in figure 1 visualizes public attitudes about changes in gender and gender relations in Mexico between 1917 and 1929. It demands neither specialized knowledge of Mexican history nor the ability to speak Spanish to decipher the dominant import of its message. The gun—a potent, universal symbol of power and violence—has been transferred from the hands of a man to those of a woman. In addition, there are other clearly identifiable meanings available to the general reader. Most of us, for example, will recognize that the 1929 woman's overall appearance—her bobbed hair, ready-to-wear dress, and stiletto shoes—signifies that she is a "modern woman," especially compared to the woman pictured in the 1917 panel. And it is not only her clothes that make her modern. We read modernity in her bold stance, her confident expression, her assured command of the gun, and her willingness to exercise her power. Most significant, the expression on the face of the man in the lower panel indicates his profound concern with the changing social landscape of gender and the apparent shift in gendered power relations.

Imagining la Chica Moderna: Women, Nation, and Visual Culture in Mexico, 1917–1936 considers the appearance of modern femininity in the everyday life of postrevolutionary culture. The book's focus on popular images of embodied gender is intended to emphasis the place and importance of the visual in the project of modernization in Mexico during the first three decades of the twentieth century.[1] The dispersion of various forms of visual culture that crossed social, cultural, and economic borders reveals the diverse range of meanings in regards to *la chica moderna*, or the modern Mexican woman, that were available to many different audiences in Mexico, not just those who lived in the sprawling neighborhoods of Mexico City. By the 1920s, the material culture of the global marketplace was spreading across the nation, addressing women in Guadalajara, Mérida, and Veracruz. Moreover, the images that Mexican women confronted were transnational and unfamiliar, as well as national, local, and familiar.

Images of the nation were bound up in a two-decade-long political and cultural effort to fashion a national citizen and promote national solidarity among diverse elements of the Mexican population. At the same time that governmental agents and intellectual elites made use of visual images to promote their version of a political modernity, an equally forceful campaign to advance a modern identity was forged in the sphere of a popular "transnational" culture situated in the marketplace. The images I look at were public and popular, reproduced mechanically and widely circulated to a heterogeneous public. In general, the production and use of these images were governed by institutional parameters — those of mass publishing, for example — and by popular aesthetic practices and genres. Some were addressed directly to women through advertisements and as illustrations accompanying articles in women's magazines and on the "woman's pages" in a variety of daily newspapers. Others illustrated domestic and international news stories, promoted tourism, or publicized the latest Mexican and Hollywood films. They were, for the most part, photographs and reprinted lithographs, the two most widely used mechanical means of image reproduction in the first decades of the twentieth century.

an up to date woman

2. *La chica moderna,*
Ilustrado, 7 March 1929, 26.

La chica moderna pictured in the cartoon in figure 2 shares a number of qualities with modern women in Europe and in the United States. She is "up-to-date" in her appearance, her dress, and her attitudes. At home she wears a mass-produced housedress covered by an apron. In the evenings, she favors slinky black evening dresses, New York and Paris fashions that barely cover her knees, and French berets that snuggly fit her short new bob. She is middle class, tall, and slender; she smokes cigarettes and wears makeup. She is the personification of feminine elegance and Parisian chic. This resemblance can be linked to the transnational distribution of the ideologies and commodities of style and fashion. While images of la chica moderna were produced and consumed within the complex context of powerful and strongly voiced nationalistic discourses, their presentational iconography was specifically that of global modernity. At the same time, the modern Mexican woman was not merely a carbon copy of her U.S., British, and German sisters, a "flapper" who spoke Spanish. An intriguing blend of traditionalism—"the china poblana" (rural woman) and the *rebozo*-wrapped Indian—and cosmopolitanism—French berets and Spanish mantillas—distinguished her from those other modern, Western women.

The book is not a social history of Mexican women; my study of popular images is not intended to show how people actually lived their lives. Instead, I offer an analysis of the production of ideas about the new postrevolutionary Mexican woman as she was envisioned in popular culture and consider how these images contributed to an understanding of Mexican modernity. As the subsequent chapters make clear, la chica moderna was, to a large extent, white—as opposed to mestizo or Indian—and middle to upper class. In Mexico, the idea of "middle class" needs to be situated within the sociopolitical context of Mexico's postrevolutionary project, which saw as its goal the transformation of Mexico from an agriculturally dependent, rural-based economy—distinguished by linguistic, class, racial, and historical divisions, and vaguely connected through regional and ancestral ties—into a modern nation populated by national citizens. The project was marked by a profound tension between the impetus to develop a homogeneous "Mexican" national identity and an equally compelling impulse to be "modern" within the transnational sense of modernity.

I use the term *transnational* here to refer to a set of economic, sociopolitical, cultural, and interpersonal forces that link states, institutions, and people across geographic and political boundaries. Of course, Mexico's encounter with the transnational did not begin in the twentieth century: the geographic region that came to be known as "Mexico" was modernized in the fifteenth century with arrival of the Spanish, who brought with them Western religious beliefs and practices, political, economic, and familial structures, as well as modern fashion. From the time of the Spanish colonization, Mexico looked to Europe as the model of modern life and modern identity, a model that was presented and interpreted initially by the envoys of the Spanish monarchy and the Catholic Church and later by French, Italian, and U.S. arbiters of modernity. Despite centuries of foreign rule and political and economic imperialism, however, the "heart and mind" of Mexico was never wholly subjugated. From the sixteenth century until the present moment, Mexican women and men have fashioned themselves national and individual

(margin notes:) definition chica moderna—White instead of mestizo

transnational

how they became modern

identities from an assemblage of images and ideas that were and are foreign and indigenous, modern and traditional. In the words of Serge Gruzinski, Mexico has always been "a land of all syncretisms" (5).

As we will see, la chica moderna was, herself, a hybrid creature. Broadly speaking, she can be understood to encompass a set of discourses employed to describe a gendered social subject that was construed to be fundamentally different from previous categories of women by virtue of being "modern." These particular discourses were bound up with those of nationalism as promoted by the state, and by private market interests whose projects sometimes coincided with national concerns and sometimes did not. Domesticity and its attendant structures of marriage and motherhood, as well as the topics of fashion and beauty, formed the primary contexts of this new image of the Mexican woman. She was first of all middle or upper class; she married for love, took care of the house and the children, and was the family's primary consumer in the marketplace; she attended church regularly and, once married, remained faithful to her husband; rarely did she work outside the home yet she participated in public–policy making, especially in the area of education and moral reform.[2]

Various histories have been written about Mexico's postrevolutionary political, cultural, and social transformations. Most of these histories are concerned with the creation of the modern Mexican state and the institutionalization of a particular "postrevolutionary" brand of nationalism represented by a set of formal symbols and discourses of *lo mexicano*, a profoundly "Mexican" national identity. They rely on written historical evidence housed in official state and private archives: presidential papers; official edicts and proclamations; letters from one political official to another; records of licenses, marriages, divorces, and death. As feminist historians have noted, however, the understanding of history as primarily *political* history has ignored histories of gender and the role of everyday practice in the formation of new national and social identities.[3]

Theorists of nationalism have for the most part been "gender blind" in their analyses. Nira Yuval-Davis insists, however, that women are central to imagining the nation and nationalism in five ways: as agents of biological reproduction, as reproducers of ethnic and national boundaries, as transmitters of national culture, as symbols of national ideologies, and as participants in national struggles (7).[4] Much of the recent scholarly work on Mexican women during the revolutionary and postrevolutionary period, roughly 1910 through 1936, focuses on one or more of these processes by looking, for example, at relations between women and social and political projects carried out by the state or other social institutions such as the Catholic Church and labor organizations. Studies examine women's participation in the Mexican revolution as *soldaderas*; their involvement in national and regional postrevolutionary political movements, and in health and education projects; or women working in factories and agriculture, and as prostitutes on the streets of Mexico City.[5]

Recently, scholars have turned to culture as a site of mediation in the construction of Mexican nationalism, recognizing that contemporary national projects are intricately bound up with twentieth-century consumer culture and with everyday practice of ordinary citizens.[6] While acknowledging the political and the economic, these studies situate cultural practices and processes at the center of their narratives rather than at the periphery. Yet, like the more traditional histories, these newer cultural histories are mostly concerned with the role of culture in the formation and affirmation of *mexicanidad*, the term given to describe an "official" postrevolutionary Mexican national identity produced through concerted political efforts. Like all contemporary national identities, this one was denoted by a set of prescripts that included a common history connecting the past to the present, and monuments and festivals commemorating that past; a national language and a set of national values; and such cultural objects and practices as songs, dances, and costumes.

There is a significant body of literature that examines a range of official projects undertaken by the state to revisualize the nation and to create a national image that could be marketed domestically and internationally. These studies' central object of analysis is the national artistic movement of the 1920s and '30s exemplified by Mexican muralism, social realism, and primitivism. Artists associated with these schools—such as Diego Rivera, David Alfaro Siqueiros, and José Clemente Orozco—practiced their art in the service of social transformation, often times under the largesse of the national government itself. Concurrently, Mexican citizens were being offered other kinds of modern identities through popular culture, advertising, illustrated magazines, comic books, and movies that were not always in agreement with the state's vision. These different representations were, in part, due to Mexico's place in the global network of economic and cultural relations and to the flow of cultural products and practices across national borders.

Conventional political history draws a picture in which the state, the market, and modern cultural institutions operated "in tandem" to create a modern citizen. While there were mutually supportive and beneficial relationships between governmental and political formations and processes and cultural, market-driven practices, there were also unavoidable tensions. These were triggered by the conflict of two ideologies that can be defined as "the ideology of collectivism" on the part of the state, versus "the ideology of individualism" on the part of the market forces. Popular culture negotiated this divide, drawing on existing practices and ideologies while at the same time producing new ones. It is precisely this heterogeneity that allows popular culture to address the dreams and desires of diverse audiences even as it is often absorbed into national hegemonic projects.

Popular culture — broadly understood to encompass all aspects of material culture and practices that are part of people's everyday lives — is a crucial site for understanding the often marginalized position of women. The concept of "everyday life" has had a particular urgency in recent cultural and historical studies of modernity. Theories of the "everyday" are interested in ordinary activities: cooking, cleaning, sleeping, walking, activities that are ordered by routine and habit. But, as Michel de Certeau has noted, even mundane activities are purposeful in the minds of people who undertake them. It is this sense of "purposefulness" that makes everyday life a social and political life. While I agree with Henri Lefebvre that "everyday life weighs heaviest on women," I take issue with his assertion that women are merely "the subject of everyday life and its victims" (1984, 73). Given the sociopolitical constraints placed on women in terms of their participation in the public sphere, the everyday is a particularly important space to examine the ways in which women actively respond to and engage with those constraints, both in the private sphere of the home and in the public sphere.

Those issues delegated to the private or woman's sphere — such as

fashion, homemaking, and child rearing — were central to the formation
of women's identity during this formative moment in Mexican history.
In this sense, the production, circulation, and use of popular culture
must be understood to be just as "political" as suffrage, education, and
working outside of the home were. In using the term *political*, I am not
suggesting that the formation of la chica moderna was in any sense a
hegemonic project directed by the state in concert with capitalist enter-
prises. In fact, in the following chapters I do not consider the successive
postrevolutionary regimes at all except where they intersect with or take
part in popular practices. Instead, in order to understand gender's political nature in the cultural construction of national and social identities, I
examine popular visual culture. I concentrate primarily on images published in illustrated magazines and daily newspapers, images reproduced
in Mexican films, and other pictorial illustrations that appeared in a
variety of genres as well as forms of popular visual culture that circulated
in the cities, towns, and villages of Mexico during the two decades that
followed the end of the Mexican revolution's military aspect. I intend
to show that ultimately Mexican women became modern not simply
through rhetoric of nationalism and an imagined conception of community, but also through their participation in transnational gendered commercial discourses and practices of everyday life.

Mexican Modernity

While there has certainly been disagreement as to the time frame of
modernity, there is consensus that it was a historical epoch that was
qualitatively different from preceding periods, marked by profound and
long-term changes in economic, political, technological, and cultural
domains. Critics now recognize that modernity was not signaled by
some momentous break between the past and the present, but was a
gradual and uneven process across and within national and geographic
boundaries. Definitions of modernity have generally focused on economic, social, and political transformations. However, recently, there
has been a turn to the question of experience and we've come to understand that for social subjects, modernity is understood to mean new ways

(margin note: Process of modernity)

of thinking about as well as a new way of experiencing the world, a "mode of vital experience" in the words of Marshall Berman. The concept of "experience" is particularly useful in that it broadens our understanding of modernity to incorporate the histories of ordinary people so that we may appreciate the ways in which individuals responded to and practiced modern life.

The process of modernity was a gradual, uneven, and often incomplete shift from a traditional, religious view of the world to a secular one. It was marked by urbanization and the rise of industrial capitalism; the invocation of scientific analysis, rationality, and material progress; and the proliferation of the "masses" and their attendant public spectacles. These ideals of material progress coexisted with appeals to the emotional and spiritual expression of individuality and a homage to the cult of individual accomplishment. In fact, the idea of the "individual" as a subjective agent is often attributed to modernity. The paradigm of individuality in turn allowed for the consideration of individual gendered identity. However, as Griselda Pollock insists, modernity "cannot function as a given category to which we add women": modernity is, among other things "organized by" and is an "organization of sexual difference" (56). Pollock's call for gender specificity and for an understanding of the gendered nature of history informs my project. The intention of this book is to analyze the gender politics of Mexican modernity by examining the ways in which women were imagined within popular visual culture during the 1920s and '30s.

(margin notes: intentions of book; analyze gender politics 1920s–1930s)

Until recently, theories and descriptions of modernity have been grounded in histories of European nations and the United States. Major philosophers of modernity talk about the modernity of Paris, Berlin, and New York, not of Rio de Janeiro, Caracas, or Mexico City. However, the various processes of contemporary modernity, the pursuit of intellectual, religious, artistic, economic, and political innovations, occurred simultaneously in Europe, the United States, and Latin America. Soon after the turn of the century, when a European version of modernity seemed to be a possibility in Latin America, the initial two-way interchange of ideas fell victim to Latin America's colonial relationship to Europe. In short, the rise of industrial capitalism in western Europe was not matched in Latin America, because of the historical condition of colonial dependency. This is not to say that Mexico and other Latin American countries did not experience modernity or that Latin American modernity was somehow "inferior" to that of Europe or the United States or deficient in some essential characteristics of a "true" experience of modernity.[7] However, it is important to recognize the specificity of national social, political, and economic projects in the formation of modern national identities.

Twentieth-century Mexican modernity is perhaps best defined by Néstor García Canclini's concept of "hybridity," which he defines as a function of "two parallel and intersecting drives": the first, motivated by the growth of the middle class and the resulting expansion of European and U.S. ideals of capitalism, liberalism, and democracy; the second, an effect of the "interweaving" of local indigenous cultures and practices with modern, global social and economic institutions (1995, 41–46). Additionally, given the high rate of illiteracy in pre- and postrevolutionary Mexico, the visual functioned as a major site through which this population could participate in modern life.[8] Processes of modernization and development in Mexico were, therefore, to a large extent, dependent on the circulation of a global visual culture. Across Latin America at the turn of the century, cultural modernity was associated with Europe — primarily France and Italy — while economic modernity was linked to the United States. By the 1920s, the cultural and economic influence of the United States surpassed that of Europe. And, while Mexico City may have been geographically closer to Rio de Janeiro or Buenos Aires, it was to New York City and Paris that modern Mexicans turned for inspiration. Mexico City's major daily newspapers featured articles addressed to and concerned with the modern woman; these articles and advertisements were illustrated with lithographs and photographs that produced a visual culture that imagined what this woman looked like.

Modernity was not an easy project in postrevolutionary Mexico. Like all versions of modernity, the Mexican experience was a product of residual and emerging social practices that spanned five decades and was interrupted by a prolonged and violent civil war, the Mexican revolution. As in other historical contexts, modernity in Mexico was marked by debate and anxiety concerning the rapidly changing role of women. The state, the church, and diverse social and political groups, as well as public intellectuals, took a keen interest in refashioning Mexican womanhood. Deliberations about new roles for women were the subject of considerable discussion in newspapers and periodicals. Journalists and public figures held forth on the shifting terrain of gender roles and relations. Articles with the titles "Women and International Peace," "Feminism: Long Live the Small Differences," "The Mexican Woman Who Murders," "The Mother as Educational Factor," "Women Who Work and Men Who Don't Work," among others, were interspersed among national, international, and local stories in major Mexico City daily newspapers such as *Excelsior* and weekly illustrated periodicals such as *El Heraldo Ilustrado* and *Revista de Revista*.

At the same time that women became more visible in the public sphere, images of women proliferated in a variety of popular mediums such as the cinema, the press, and other forms of mass media. The proliferation and diversity of these images suggest a wide-ranging attempt among various social constituencies to fashion a female subjectivity and a female body that could respond to the demands of a new sociopolitical environment that required women to be modern *and* Mexican. I argue that a historically situated examination of these very visible images of femininity will provide us with a clearer understanding of the forces that shaped ideologies of gender in postrevolutionary Mexico and of the ways in which Mexicans imagined modernity as a gendered practice.

Gender and Visual Culture

Visual culture may be defined as "those material artifacts, buildings and images, plus time-based media and performances, produced by human labour and imagination, which serve aesthetic, symbolic, ritualistic or ideological-political ends, and/or practical functions, and which address the sense of sight to a significant extent" (Walker and Chaplin, 1–2). While the study of visual culture emerged in the discipline of art history, scholars in diverse fields — anthropology, geography, history, media studies, and so forth — have more recently taken the term *visual culture* to mean almost any kind of human-made material artifact that serves aesthetic or practical functions and that is mass produced or made within a

craft or art context. The primary consideration is that such artifacts address the sense of sight. As many have argued, vision was central to
modern social and subjective formations.[9] In fact, the modern world can
be defined, in part, by the proliferation of images that flow across geographic, linguistic, temporal, cultural, and technological borders. Of
course, long before the invention of the camera, peoples' lives were filled
with various forms of figurative art that asserted references to the real
world. Paintings and sculptures filled museums, galleries, and the halls
of wealthy homes around the world; bibles and other books were illustrated with reproduced drawings and paintings; and images of fa-
mous people circulated widely. However, as the invention of the still
and motion picture camera and new kinds of technological reproduction encouraged the proliferation of visual images across national, class,
and gendered boundaries, images came to have more meaning and force
in the social construction of modern reality and in people's everyday
experience.

It is the understanding of visual culture as "productive" that informs
this book. First, images do not reflect the world; they are part of the
realm of social discourse that participates in the context of everyday life;
they are both responsive to as well as constructive of this life. Images
function as elements of discourses, providing people with information
and knowledge. At the same time, it is important to remember that the
production and reception of these images are organized within social,
institutional, and professional systems that generate their own logic.
Professional practices, aesthetic conventions, and legal and moral regulations police popular culture and limit the kinds of images available for
people to engage with. Second, visual culture is never only visual: we
experience images as part of a structure of sounds and written text that
are produced within institutional and ideological systems. And, finally,
we need to understand that visual culture is not merely a collection of
objects but also a space in which social interaction takes place, a space in
which social subjects engage with, challenge, and actively transform cultural codes.

Here, I borrow from Lefebvre's understanding of space as a "social
product," an artifact of human practice rather than "a container without
content"; it is a location in which social power is activated and social

relations are enacted. Gender and gender relations are produced through the textual and symbolic coding and occupation of historically consti- tuted spaces, and, in turn, social constructions of sexual difference orga- nize gendered spatial patterns. For example, because women were seen as keepers of home and family, the kitchen was understood to be a "feminine" space in which "feminine" practices took place. Visual cul- ture functions therefore as a kind of map of the purpose and use of space that guides people through the complex geography of everyday experi- ence. People look to images to help them make sense of reality; for suggestions on how to be in the world, how to act, to move through particular spaces, and how to dress, as well as how to relate to other individuals and material objects and spaces. In this sense, pictorial repre- sentations operate as part of the complex process of self-identification or the self-fashioning of identity.

At the same time, we must remember that images are social "things" or inanimate objects that have historically specific functions. Furthermore, their meanings are dependent on the context in which they are produced and circulated. They may be photographs illustrating a news story, an advertisement selling a commodity or service, a poster promoting a po- litical candidate, or the premiere of a new motion picture. Images adorn picture postcards purchased to send to friends and family or to add to personal collections; they're used for magazine and book covers to describe in some way what is contained inside. Finally, the institu- tional, aesthetic, and professional conventions of journalism, advertis- ing, movies, and the publishing industry determine the ways in which we "see" images.

Most important, visual culture is filtered through the eyes of individ- ual social subjects. While images provide information, they also offer "scopic," corporeal, and psychic pleasures that cannot be read through textual analysis. Viewers draw on different cultural competencies and individual desires to make images mean something to them. Individuals have learned to see the world in particular ways that have been shaped by social and individual histories. Vision and representation, the produc- tion and consumption of images, cannot be teased apart; they are inti- mately connected as part of a complex social system of signification that involves the production, circulation, and consumption of images.

Within the environment of visual culture in Mexico, "modern" female gendered subject positions and traits categorized as "feminine" were embodied in particular material figurations of the feminized body. *Imagining la Chica Moderna* is organized around the conviction that visual images of women *embody* popular discourses about sexuality, work, motherhood, and feminine beauty, as well as other social categories that intersect with gender such as class, race, and ethnicity. To "embody" a discourse literally means to make visible upon the physical body social ideas and ideologies or, in other words, to historicize the body. The process of historicizing the body involves both involuntary as well as voluntary practices. Here, it is important to understand that social ideas are not simply "imposed on the individual from the outside"; individual social subjects actively take part in the self-fashioning of a visible social identity through the selective incorporation of available "modes of self-production" (Grosz, 143–44).[10] This understanding of the body as historical as opposed to "natural" allows us to see that representations of femininity (as well as masculinity) are images of social "ideas" rather than reproductions of social facts.

In her book *The Spectacular Modern Woman: Feminine Visibility in the 1920s*, Liz Conor considers visions of modern "types" of the New Woman — the city girl, the screen star, the flapper — that "appeared" through new forms of visual technologies. Drawing on and expanding Judith Butler's work on gendered "performativity," Conor argues that while the term *appearing* could refer to performance, it also takes on a new orientation in relation to the "visual." Conor writes that appearing describes how the changed conditions of feminine visibility in modernity "invited a practice of the self which was centered on one's visual status and effects. . . . For women to identify themselves as modern, the performance of their gendered identity had to take place within the modern spectacularization of everyday life" (7). As images of modernity and the modern woman proliferated, women remade themselves by appropriating the iconography of those images. As Conor puts it, "modernity's visions of women became part of women's self-perception as modern: gendered representations became embodied" (8). *Imagining la Chica Moderna* pursues this consideration of the visual as central to modern feminine identity formation, arguing that gender's *visibility* is the reason why the study of visual culture is vital to our understanding of historical change and the modernization of gender.

I begin by asking in what way does the 1925 advertisement for the "cigarrera mexicana" Claveles in figure 3 (below) function as a historical document? For Roland Marchand, advertisements "cannot be taken as authoritative evidence of the ideas of those who heard or read them." Instead, they may be understood as traces, glimpses, or indications of popular attitudes and social realities. Additionally, they "do reveal what products and services were sold during a given era, when new products first attained mass distribution, and what explanations and suggestions were offered for their use" (2000, xviii). The Claveles advertisement that includes an image of a Mexican *flapperista* informs us, for example, that cigarette smoking was an activity that was promoted to Mexican women in the 1920s, and that advertisers imagined that the modern Mexican woman smoked and bobbed her hair. We can also see that the Mexican advertising industry utilized global understandings of modern feminin- ity and international design practices in its marketing campaigns ad- dressed to women. An analysis of the advertisement cannot, however, tell us what individual women thought of the flapperista. At most, this ad reveals cultural ideas about gender, rather than a social history of Mexican consumers. The following chapters therefore do not intend to show how people actually lived their lives or used specific commodities. Instead, this book considers how visual culture contributed to the idea of the modern Mexican woman.

Studies of visual culture from a feminist perspective situate themselves within a number of critical interpretive contexts. Some, concerned with questions of power and agency, focus on questions of individual and/or collective reception, with ways in which psychic and social processes shape consumption habits. These projects privilege questions of resis- tance and cultural agency. While not wanting to define women as lacking agency, we do need to acknowledge the real limits placed on women's bodies in order to understand ways in which they were able to resist or mediate those limits. This book, therefore, is interested in what Kathryn Shevelow calls the "intended 'reading situation' for women" (16). It begins from an assumption that consumption is, above all, a social prac- tice, rather than an individual one.

3. Advertisement for the Mexican cigarette Claveles, *Excelsior*,
14 July 1925, unpaginated.

As Shevelow reminds, "we cannot know with any degree of certainty how historically distant readers read." If the materials readers engaged with are somehow textually available to us today, what is not accessible "are those historically distant readers themselves, aside from whatever evidence may survive in letters, diaries, and essays, of how they experienced their lives, their personal and cultural histories, in their engagement with the texts they read." While Shevelow acknowledges that there "must have been readers, both women and men, who 'read against the grain,'" the best that contemporary critics can confirm from the textual remnants that remain, are areas of possible resistant reading positions available to these readers (16). Thus, an understanding of what kinds of interpretations women made of the popular images they encountered daily can only be indirectly construed through an analysis of the images within the context of available reading strategies and public discourses. The following chapters that look at images that appeared in illustrated magazines and daily newspapers, Mexican films, postcards, and tourism campaigns will serve as maps that will guide us through the visual material available to women in Mexico between 1917 and 1940, material with which they could imagine a fashion a modern female self.

Chapter 1, "Visualizing the New Nation," situates la chica moderna and popular visual culture within the political, economic, and cultural context of the emergence of postrevolutionary nationalism. I trace the rise of consumer capitalism that was accompanied by the expansion of popular visual culture in the form of illustrated magazines, advertising, and the motion picture industry. Chapter 2, "*En México como en París*: Fashioning *la Chica Moderna*," examines the relationship between fashion, modernity, and female identity in Mexico. I consider the emergent role of advertising in reflecting fashion as "an aspect of women's negotiation of modernity and post-traditional identity" within the context of twentieth-century consumer culture (Berry, xii–xiii). In examining transnational marketing strategies and discourses of fashion that shaped a public understanding of la chica moderna, I consider the influence of Hollywood and Paris in promoting modern fashion.

Chapter 3, "Domesticating *la Chica Moderna*," considers how discourses of modernity and ideals of the modern housewife were promoted through visual culture to Mexican women. Specifically, I examine the role of advertising within the context of the changing notions of domesticity in the postwar years. These discourses advised women about contemporary progressive child-rearing theories and encouraged them to fill their modern homes with the latest in furniture design and cooking and cleaning gadgets. Chapter 4, "Picturing Working Women," investigates the idea of working women as represented in illustrated magazines and newspapers and Mexican cinema. The chapter looks at images of working women in order to determine to what extent these images participated in the discursive reconsideration of modern womanhood and femininity. Chapter 5, "*La Moda Mexicana*: Exotic Women," examines folkloric and traditional images of female "types" such as *la china poblana* and *La Tehuana*, which came to define the "domestic exotic," an alternative form of modern femininity made available to Mexican women. Finally, the conclusion, "Imagining 'Real' Mexican Women," examines the visual representation of "real" women as epitomized in photographs that accompanied articles about Mexico City's "social scene," crime stories, and media stories regarding the political and cultural contribution of women across Mexico during the 1920s and '30s. This chapter also considers the possible relation between the "real" and the "imagined" and asks in what ways these two realms came together in the production of la chica moderna.

Chapter 1

Visualizing the New Nation

Santa (directed by Antonio Moreno, 1931), based on a novel published in 1903 by Federico Gamboa, and one of the first successful Mexican sound films, narrates the tragedy of a young peasant girl, abandoned by her lover, who escapes to Mexico City to avoid the wrath of her brothers.[1] The transition from the film's prologue, set in the rural village of Chimalistac, to Santa's arrival in Mexico City illustrates her entrance into the space of modernity. The film's, and Santa's, introduction to the city presents the idea that urban modernity was "overstimulating" to millions of rural migrants who poured into Mexico City during the first few decades of the new century. The deliberate juxtaposition of the ordered, uncluttered, immobile "premodern" rural landscape with the scene of modern urban life marked by a visual and aural intensity, an overabundance of stimuli, and a formless and crowded discontinuity, is visualized through the female body: a fade-to-black from an image of Santa lying in the dust of Chimalistac as her lover rides off with his troops is followed by a fade-in to a montage of "technologies of amusement" — a spinning game wheel, a Ferris wheel, and a merry-go-round.

The optical effect itself serves as a metaphor for historical, social, and cinematic change. Through the technology of the modern cinema, Santa's body is aligned with the mechanical body that is representative of modern life as both woman and the cinema become modern. The use of a static camera and immobile framing in the prologue is replaced by a moving camera and mobile composition while the melodramatic acting style of silent film gives way to a more realist technique. As the film fades up from black, a sequence of documentary-style footage shot with a hand-held, moving camera reveals the crowd of modern life moving as one body through a bustling urban marketplace, the symbol of commodified modern space.

We can begin to make out that this crowd is composed of individuals: some are clothed in modern dress, others wear the traditional clothing of their village; women with bobbed hair and cloche hats mingle with those adorned in long braids tied with ribbons, and men in suits rub shoulders with Indians in the peasant's uniform of white pants and shirt. It is a stark image of the modern, postrevolutionary Mexican nation that is made up of new and old, middle class and working class, traditional and contemporary modes of being. This scene also emphasizes the "sensational" aspect of modern urban life, or, more precisely, the overload of sensory stimulus that modern citizens are exposed to. The camera's point of view simulates what it is like to move through the multitude, a mass of bodies that moves as if it is a single giant organism. The camera glances here and there at the mix of social characters brought together in the modern city. Finally, it rests on Santa's face and registers her expression of shock and wonder at her first encounter with the intensity and discontinuity of modernity.

At the end the nineteenth century, Mexico City enjoyed the reputation of a cosmopolitan, European-style urban center. Porfirio Díaz, the army general who seized power in Mexico in 1876, was intent on the modernization of Mexico through the philosophy of liberal positivism, a Mexican version of the Enlightenment that promoted the logic of rationality and science as the motor of progress. The object of Díaz and his supporters, *los científicos* as they were called — a privileged group of businessmen and political intellectuals — was to modernize Mexico under a banner of "peace, order, and progress" through the mechanisms of capitalism and rational management. Their influences were the global discourses of social Darwinism and the neoliberal philosophies of the French sociologist Auguste Comte. Under Díaz (1876–1910), Mexico enjoyed political and economic stability, rising wages, a booming population growth, and the ascendancy of an entrepreneurial middle class.

With a population in 1895 of approximately 330,000, Mexico City presented itself to the world as a vibrant cosmopolitan urban center. Stately historic government buildings that circled the Zócalo, or city center, celebrated the city's colonial heritage; ornate mansions and modern *colonias* (residential housing developments), erected in the neighborhoods conjoining the Zócalo, housed the wealthy and the rising middle class; picturesque horse-drawn carriages shared the street with the occasional automobile; and fashionably dressed women spent their afternoons strolling the main artery, the Paseo de la Reforma, perusing the aisles of modern department stores, such as the Compaña Mercantil. This elegant facade, however, could not entirely cover up the underbelly of modernity. Millions of migrants from impoverished rural areas flooded city streets, selling food, crafts, and their labor. On the east side of the Zócalo, one would encounter overcrowded and unsanitary dwellings, disease, and unpaved streets covered in garbage and waste.[2] If the wealthy landowning and bourgeois classes enjoyed the fruits of economic expansion, the lives of the majority of Mexicans stagnated as most were locked into a system of debt peonage or low industrial wages.

Most economic historians agree that structural changes that ensued during the reign of Díaz were due primarily to economic and political policies that liberalized trade, redistributed property, and nationalized a number of industries. The policies of Díaz's administration favored the urban entrepreneurial class and the mining and manufacturing sectors, even though 80 percent of the population was rural and "seldom entered the market economy" (Hansen, 24).[3] An unprecedented migration of rural peasants into industrializing urban centers led to an emerging low-wage proletariat class who worked in Mexican industry's expanding production sectors, such as textiles, steel manufacturing, and mining. Between 1895 and 1910, Mexico City experienced a population increase of 50 percent.

One statistic often overlooked is that, according to census data, the majority of migrants to the capital — 53 percent — were women (Lear, 52–54). The lives of all women, regardless of their social status, changed significantly during this period. For example, while married women remained under the control of their husbands, unmarried women gained new social civil rights. Additionally, the changes engendered by the industrial revolution and the increase in the mass production of goods once manufactured at home, meant that middle- and upper-class women no longer had to work alongside their husbands to maintain the hacienda. Domesticity and motherhood became full-time occupations. Women of the moneyed classes were able to take advantage of increased access to education through an expansion of public education, and they entered male-gendered fields of business, teaching, nursing, and politics (Soto, 5). A young woman named L. Josefina Reyes insisted in 1903 that "our period of progress and of struggle has opened a wide field where one can struggle for life, to improve her intellectual and moral power, which is not inferior to that of man" (quoted in Vallens, 20).

Lower-class women also experienced the effects of Díaz's social and economic policies, albeit in a very different way. Displaced from their work in the fields of the haciendas, many migrated to Mexico City and other urban centers looking for work. They found jobs in textile and cigar manufacturing; worked as domestics and as clerks in small shops and offices; and earned wages in clothing and textile factories as *costureras*, or seamstresses. Some industrious women became entrepreneurs in the "unofficial" market as street vendors and tortilla makers. Many turned to prostitution out of desperation or because they found that they could earn more money in that profession than in any other.[4] Despite their more limited economic and social opportunities, working-class women were also exposed to the same modern ideas as their more affluent sisters, and, if they could not purchase the *haute couture* on display in the department store window, they could at least admire those fashions.

The history of twentieth-century modernity and the modern Mexican is unquestionably tied to the massive social, cultural, and economic upheaval brought about by the unrelenting seven-year span of hostilities known as the Mexican revolution (1911–17). This upheaval was largely a social and cultural rebellion that was responding to the Porfiriato's suppression of local autonomy and labor organizing, and its refusal to take on the responsibility of social reform. While the middle and upper classes enjoyed a brief period of economic boom, the majority of Mexicans never realized monetary or lifestyle benefits. The national population doubled, real wages dropped, and the standard of living for Mexico's poorest remained stagnant and impoverished. To make matters worse, a nationwide agriculture disaster precipitated by the collapse of the sugar industry, a famine in central and northern Mexico, and a severe drop in corn production initiated a severe economic crisis beginning in 1907 (Smith, 163–64).

Widespread economic problems, such as the rising cost of food and other necessities and the resulting increase in peasant and labor unrest, eventually led to the outbreak of armed conflict. In actuality, the hostilities cannot be viewed as a single, organized insurgency in the manner of the French or Soviet revolutions. Instead, Mexicanists have argued that the Mexican revolution was actually a "collection of intertwined *revolutions*" that included "the old regime . . . the liberal opposition, largely urban and heavily middle class . . . [and] the popular movement, essentially rural and peasant in composition" (Knight 1990, 227).[5] Moreover, the conclusion of the armed conflict in 1917 did not bring about resolution among these factions. Instead, the following decade was disrupted by continuing political dissension that occasionally escalated into armed insurgency as in the case of the Cristero Revolt (1926–29), a Catholic rebellion fought at a cost of 80,000 lives.

Despite large-scale social and economic transformations, the shift from the prerevolutionary Porfirian regime to postrevolutionary nationalism cannot be categorized as a movement from tradition to modernity. Instead, this period may be understood as an accelerated shift from one kind of modernizing project to another. Because of the complexity of social and economic ideologies that instigate this civil strife, the group that emerged after 1915 to govern Mexico was an amalgamation made up of the three "major historical actors" of the revolution: the old Porfirian regime; the urban, middle-class liberal opposition; and the rural popular movement. More significantly, unlike the Soviet Revolution in which class conflict was central, the transformation wrought by the Mexican Revolution and its aftermath were, to a large degree, cultural. The seemingly contradictory nature of postrevolutionary national policies supported the rising middle class and capitalist development on one hand, and advocated a populist rhetoric that lobbied for agrarian reform and the rights of the campesino on the other.[6]

A concerted political and cultural process that promoted an idealized revolutionary rhetoric, together with a shared mythologized history of conquest and colonization, molded a national sentiment that united a diverse and divided population. During these two decades, political and cultural nationalism was at the forefront of intellectual and cultural discourse. The central project of the nationalist campaign was the consolidation and amplification of a coherent national identity and the promotion of nationalistic sentiment. This project came up against a number of different historical practices, which included indigenous traditions and structures; religious Catholic traditions and structures; and modern, Western discourses and economic and social structures. The state was involved not merely in constructing a new political formation but also in instituting a new cultural ethos, new social relationships, and social practices that would support a modern citizen. The challenge faced by various postrevolutionary administrations was to unite a radically diverse population, divided by centuries of racial, ethnic, class, and regional allegiances (Knight 1990, 228). Additionally, Mexico faced critical problems of internal migration, labor unrest, unemployment, factional discord, as well as continuing regional revolts and religious conflicts. The state quickly understood that its goal would be achieved not through coercion and repression but through the establishment of a hegemonic populist consensus.

Despite the fact that the state-initiated national project was never totalizing, and that competing and resistant discourses emerged, people divided by regional affiliations, linguistic and ethnic differences, and religious and political beliefs came to identify themselves as Mexican. Although initialized through the will of a powerful political and intellectual elite, the myth of a historically shared understanding of what it meant to be Mexican could not have inserted itself so successfully in the national consciousness unless it somehow engaged the public in this process. Rural Indians and mestizos who migrated to the cities brought their tribal and familial religious and cultural traditions, social values, and familial and gender roles and relationships. They responded to and engaged with modernity differently than those who had been living urban lives for a few generations. Diverse groups mingled in public city spaces of the marketplace, cantinas, and churches, forming new kinds of political and social alliances. While directives on how to be a new Mexican issued from the requirements of the new social order, the eventual adoption or rejection of Mexican nationalism emanated from people's responses to and experiences with profound transformations in their daily lives. Ultimately, the new citizen was an ambiguous figure who, on one hand, lived and worked in the countryside with family or with people he had known all his life. On the other hand, she was also urban and resided in crowded neighborhoods with unknown and unrelated people, worked in factories or public service, and was a consumer and a producer of goods and services. Regardless of where this new "ideal" citizen lived, however, the nationalist campaign identified the citizen with the nation, rather than with a village, a neighborhood, an extended family, an occupation, or a particular racial or ethnic heritage.

At a material level, the war and its effects (disease and migration, for example) decimated the population of Mexico as a whole. At the same time, the population of Mexico City doubled due primarily to the migration of inhabitants from other states into the city center (Piccato, 21).[7] Piccato points to two interesting and overlooked factors: First, not all of the migrants were uneducated peasants; second, "migration to Mexico City also distinguished itself from that of other areas of the country in that the sex ratio favored women" so that by 1930 women made up more than 55 percent of the population (22). While the Mexican Constitution of 1917 institutionalized many traditional gendered practices, it did address the rights of women in a number of significant ways: it mandated public primary education for girls as well as boys, instituted protective legislation regarding women and child labor, authorized women the right to initiate divorce, and gave women a number of legal rights in the public sphere of commerce.

Additionally, the state implemented various social projects aimed at women in rural and urban areas that were concerned with transforming child rearing, as well as health and hygiene practices. Along with providing needed services such as postnatal health care and sending teachers to rural villages, social initiatives were also intent on revolutionizing social behavior in order to bring campesinos into the twentieth century. The ideology that informed these initiatives attests to the state's paternalistic attitude toward its agrarian populations.

An increased access to public education and the spread of national literacy campaigns meant that more and more people could now read and write.[8] Hundreds of newspapers, weekly journals, and popular fiction genres emerged to meet the demands of the explosion in literacy rates so that by 1935, "nearly a thousand periodicals were being published in Mexico" (Bartra, 305). In addition, motion pictures, radio, and other forms of public mass entertainment appeared in small towns and big cities, bringing even illiterate citizens images and ideas from around the world that included new notions about gender and gender relations.

As early as 1830, illustrated magazines and daily newspapers were dispersing the printed image to readers and nonreaders alike. Illustrated covers (see figure 4), engravings, and photographs that accompanied news stories and other kinds of articles communicated social values and ideas to a heterogeneous public who participated in this visual culture in a variety of ways. Although the majority of popular illustrated magazines published in Mexico propagated a consistent set of dominant social ideologies, we can't ignore the fact that middle-class, working-class, and rural Mexicans engaged with these images within the larger context of their individual needs and desires as well as through divergent categories of taste and social values.

The technology of photoengraving was introduced into the Mexican press at the end of the nineteenth century. Photographs and lithographic illustrations made their appearance soon after, during the first decade of the twentieth century as the proliferation of magazines aimed at general and particular publics increased. The introduction of illustrated magazines such as *Artes y Letras* and *La Semana Ilustrada* widened the circulation and reception of photographic images, especially for the large segment of the Mexican public that was illiterate (Debroise, 182). Mexican photographers documented political events across the nation for the

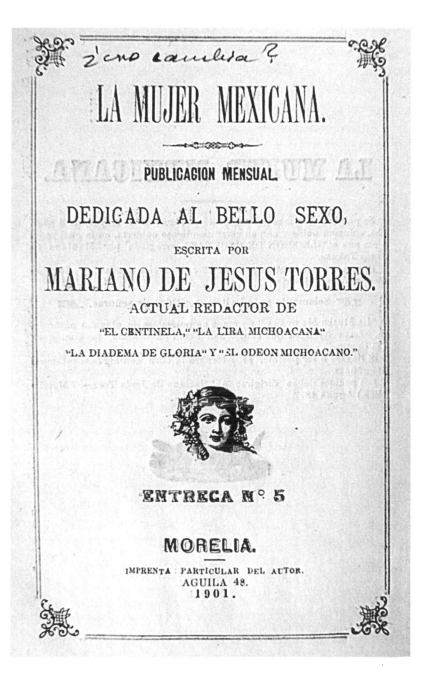

LA MUJER MEXICANA.

PUBLICACION MENSUAL.

DEDICADA AL BELLO SEXO,

ESCRITA POR

MARIANO DE JESUS TORRES.

ACTUAL REDACTOR DE

"EL CENTINELA," "LA LIRA MICHOACANA"

"LA DIADEMA DE GLORIA" Y "EL ODEON MICHOACANO."

ENTREGA N.º 5

MORELIA.

IMPRENTA PARTICULAR DEL AUTOR.

AGUILA 48.

1901.

4. Cover of the February 1901 edition of *La Mujer Mexicana*.

largely illiterate population. In 1911, the photographer Agustín Víctor Casasola, opened Casasola's Agencia Fotográfica Mexicana and hired photographers to document revolutionary battles around the country (Mraz, 2004, 24). These images appeared in the press and were also reproduced as postcards. In fact, Oliver Debroise suggests that "postcards . . . were at least as important as the press" in disseminating images of battles and of heroes such as Madero, Zapata, and Pancho Villa (178).⁹ After the revolution, photographs were used more widely by advertisers as they became less expensive to acquire and reproduce, and, more important, photography was associated with "the new," with a sense of "authenticity," and with the concept of "sincerity" because of its perceived relation to reality. Commercial photographers, inspired by the aesthetics of art photography, employed stylistic techniques associated with camera angles, choice of lenses, the use of light and shadow, and the construction of modern art backdrops in order to convey style, to inspire emotion, and to link their work with contemporary aesthetic discourses (Marchand 1995, 149–53).

Gender was a popular visual subject in both the political and the commercial spheres. Images of gendered bodies were marshaled in support of the rearticulation of postrevolutionary nationalism. One significant example was the centerpiece of the Mexican Pavilion at the 1929 World's Fair in Seville, Spain, a narrative mural by the Mexican artist Víctor Reyes. According to Mauricio Tenorio-Trillo's description, Reyes's mural was divided into two parts, the masculine side and the feminine side. The description of the mural by the Pavilion's architect, Manuel Amabilis, asserted that the masculine side represented "concepts and activities that attempt to implant ideals, create beauty, and perfect the human species." The feminine side, on the other hand, denoted "practical, immediately obtainable concepts . . . [because] those ideals of immense scope but difficult to secure are reserved for men" (quoted in Tenorio-Trillo, 230). As Mauricio Tenorio-Trillo puts it, the pavilion "condensed a relatively complete image of a revolutionary, more or less populist, modern, and virile Mexico" (231). In this sense, the underlying patriarchal structure of Mexican society remained unchanged in spite of massive economic and social revolutionary reforms. In fact, as a number of writers have noted, machismo, the historically specific form of Mexican patriarchy, served as a central theme of the revolution for decades as the state sought to consolidate the opposing revolutionary ideologies of peasant and working classes, the *pequeña burguesía*, and the wealthy landowners. An especially visible case in point was the erection of statues of revolutionary heroes across Mexico that commemorated the valiant champions of the revolution — Francisco Madero, Venustiano Carranza, Emiliano Zapata, and Francisco "Pancho" Villa.[10]

"Revolutionary machismo" was part of a two-decade period in which successive administrations promoted versions of a nationalist campaign to mold a modern nation and a coherent national identity that came to be known as *mexicanidad*. Mexicanidad was formed and solidified through a set of discourses, stereotypes, myths, and histories that were disseminated through state-controlled public education and through numerous official cultural projects that included the painting of huge murals in public places and the building of monuments to the revolution's heroes, as noted above. José Vasconcelos, minister of education under President Alvaro Obregón, commissioned Mexican artists such as David Alfaro Siqueiros, Diego Rivera, and José Clemente Orozco to create murals honoring the "heroes" of the revolution on the walls of numerous public buildings. Rivera produced a series of murals for the Ministry of Education between 1923 and 1928, while Siqueiros painted *Burial of a Worker* and *Call to Liberty* at the Escuela Nacional Preparatoria.[11]

However, the emergence of a postrevolutionary Mexican nation and national identity was not merely a product of state myth-making and engineering. Historians of this period of Mexican history argue that cultural transformation in the period immediately following the end of the military phase of the revolution emerged from changes in economic sectors, rather than from outright political legislating, and that economic power was a central component to the success of postrevolutionary regimes.[12] The spread of nationalism coincided with an exponential expansion in the marketplace that was dominated by the United States and Europe, who were concerned that Mexico might attempt to assert "national control over foreign investments"; thus they pushed for open-market reforms (Smith, xi).[13] Although Mexicans in general resented the continuing influence of the United States on the Mexican economy and culture, this relationship was central to economic expansion in Mexico.

Ultimately, open-market reforms were encouraged by the Mexican state in the hope that it would benefit Mexican business interests (69–73).

During the Porfiriato, Mexico depended on the investment of American capital to support the building of a modern infrastructure.[14] This relationship was reinforced throughout the 1920s, encouraged by Mexican and U.S. businessmen with the support of both the Mexican and U.S. governments. As a consequence, the U.S. government recognized Plutarco Elías Calles as "the best president the country has had since Díaz" (quoted in Hamilton, 74). As a result of this economic expansion, capitalism in Mexico was transformed (as it was all over the world) into a cultural system of consumption that was tied to social status and class, and to gender.

The preeminent project of the state and of political, intellectual, and business leaders was the modernization of the economy. At the end of the nineteenth century, Mexico had a limited consumer society, which can be defined as a society in which the production, circulation, and buying and selling of goods is carried out within the structure of capitalist exchange systems.[15] The emergence of a consumer society in Latin America was grounded in its neocolonial relationship with Europe and the United States. Although Spanish and other colonizing forces initially imposed commodities and ideologies upon their colonies, by the middle of the nineteenth century Latin Americans were actively acquiring foreign-made goods in order to construct themselves as "less 'barbarous,' more 'civilized,' more 'modern,' or more *de onda*, more 'with it'" (Bauer, 9). During this period, a small but expanding group of "middling consumers," who would eventually be defined as middle class, "sought through consumption and behavior to distinguish themselves from the unwashed rural mass while groping for marriage and membership in the still essentially white elite" (133). A manual addressed to "middling consumers" in Mexico, *Manual de urbanidad y buenas maneras*, written by Manuel Antonio Carreña, first published in 1853, then brought out in countless revised editions over fifty years, provided "rules for membership in the new, modernizing liberal order" (134–35).

In response to the rising demand for foreign commodities, more and more goods made in Europe and the United States appeared in department stores and neighborhood markets. As in other parts of the modernizing world, the proliferation of consumer products engendered an explosion in advertising. Advertising emerged as central to the promotion of consumption by providing information about products and services, assigning those products symbolic significance while defining use and value, and working to create and channel consumer desire for these products. It has been argued, in fact, that the primary economic function of advertising, is to "manufacture desire" in the service of the culture of consumption. Advertisers advocated consumption, the purchasing and utilization of material goods, as a means toward self-realization or the fashioning of a self that could be conveyed to others.[16]

At the end of the nineteenth century, large companies specializing in home and beauty commodities changed their advertising strategy and began developing organized and systematic campaigns to create demand for new products. Historical analyses of advertising find that by the 1920s, however, advertisers had switched from product branding to target marketing. Moreover, as consumption was increasingly conceived of as a feminine practice, the U.S. advertising industry characterized its primary target audience as "female in gender" regardless of class. Magazines — especially women's magazines — turned from subscriptions and sales to advertising for their main source of income, providing advertisers with an unlimited supply of potential consumers (Garvey, 9). Compare, for example, the 1916 advertisement for "el horno 'ideal,'" with a 1932 ad promoting "Veramon," a headache tablet especially made for the modern woman. The ad for the ideal oven (figure 5) is addressed to a faceless, genderless consumer; the image and the text focus solely on the attributes of the product itself, informing the reader that it is very strong and economical, that it can be operated with either coal or electrical power, and that it is the best product on the market. Conversely, the ad for Veramon tablets (figure 6), made especially for the "feminine organism," speaks directly to *la mujer moderna*, pictured at the wheel of her car, whose independent and busy life leaves her no time for aches and pains.

Modern print ads such as the one for Veramon tablets represented social experiences that endorsed certain kinds of feminized roles, activities, and occupations. Women were pictured as, first of all, consumers, concerned with buying fashions for themselves and products for

EL HORNO "IDEAL"

Es el único que sirve para usarse
CON CARBON O CON ELECTRICIDAD.

Para usarse con electricidad tiene CUATRO DISTINTAS TEMPERATURAS, y para emplearse con carbón basta ponerlo sobre cualquiera hornilla del brasero, sin peligro de que sufra su mecanismo eléctrico. En una u otra forma desarrolla un calor uniforme y cuece preciosamente toda clase de panes y alimentos en general. Es muy violento y económico en gasto de corriente. Su precio es más bajo que el de aparatos muy inferiores en construcción y utilidad.

Tengo Hornillas Eléctricas Infundibles y de Todos Precios.
"LA COCINA IDEAL"
2a. Nuevo México No. 38.
Teléfonos: Eric. 6879. Mex. 6717 Rojo.

5. "El horno 'ideal.'" (The ideal oven), *El Hogar* 2 December 1916, unpaginated.

their family and homes. But at the same time, the typical woman was also pictured at the wheel of her car, independent, in charge of her life, and actively pursuing new kinds of social identities. The "women's pages" of a 1911 issue of the Mexican woman's periodical, *Femina*, included an article entitled "La señorita en la calle" (The Young Woman on the Street), that advised single women that they no longer had to lower their eyes when they encountered men on the boulevards of Mexico City. On the same page, there appeared an illustration of a "modelo parisiense," the prototype of the modern new woman, dressed in the latest fashion from Paris that was available in Mexican shops and department stores.

The purpose of advertisements, of course, was not to depict "real life" but to sell products and to market the idea of consumption as a positive social and individual good.[17] If advertising provided information about

6. Speaking to the "modern woman," *Excelsior*, 1 May 1932, unpaginated.

the availability and use of new products, it also worked to train people to conceive of needs that could only be satisfied by buying things. Through dressing in a particular way, buying a modern washing machine or automobile, or smoking a particular brand of cigarette, a consumer could refashion herself in the "image" of the modern woman presented in advertisements. Consumption thus offered women a chance to actively take part in marking out their own material practices in the home and in the world, while at the same time the housewife's industry and creativity would be "properly" marshaled in the service of home and family.

Advertisements were introduced into magazines in the 1890s, and by the 1910s most popular magazines contained ads whose placement was designed to break up the stories and articles, inviting women to imagine themselves wearing "trajes estilo sastre" or "las últimas creaciones de

7. *Planchas eléctricas*, *El Hogar*, 1 November 1916.

París." While the first advertising agency in Mexico opened its doors in 1905 and advertising revenue quadrupled between 1910 and 1922, "advertising was not a high priority among Mexican businesses" (Moreno 2003, 25).[18] A glance through the major Mexican newspapers and magazines shows that the majority of advertisements during the first few decades of the century promoted American- and European-made products, while Mexican advertising publicized local shops and services. An ad for a Mexico City store called Electromoto, S.A., in the 1 November 1916 edition of the magazine *El Hogar* offered "electric flat irons — of the best American standard" (figure 7). Housewives could buy "Bon Ami" at any of the major drugstores and hardware stores in Mexico City. Colgate Ribbon Dental Cream and Flytox insecticide were sold all over the city, thanks to José Uihlein and Associates (*Revista de Revista*, 3 January 1926, 9). And "la mujer moderna" could purchase Johnson & Johnson's Modess feminine napkins in any drugstore (*Ilustrado*, 31 October 1920, 43).

   If you wandered through one of Mexico City's largest department stores, such as Casa Boker, you'd find that most of the products on display and listed in the store's catalogue were produced in Europe or the United States (Buchenau, 46).[19] The preponderance of European and American commodities helped create an understanding of modernity as being, above all, foreign. This understanding proved a powerful force in the shaping of popular images of *la chica moderna*. Thus, while the visual iconography of modernity as pictured in advertising addressed to Mexican women in the 1920s and 1930s needs to be situated within the specific historical condition of postrevolutionary cultural politics, because of the transnational nature of advertising, it must also be considered as part of a phenomenon that circulated across national borders. Although advertisements spoke to women in Spanish and may have referred to ideals of national gendered identities, their iconography and aesthetics evidence the globalizing aspect of modernity and the concurrent ideology of middle-class domesticity.

Women and Visual Culture

Magazines addressed to women were introduced in Europe in the eighteenth century, providing a new public space for women, a space that helped to produce a new kind of female community. In Great Britain, the *Lady's Magazine*, the *Female Spectator*, and the *Lady's Weekly Magazine* included literary excerpts, articles intended to improve the moral life of women, and essays about various topics — with titles such as "Philosophy," "Geography," "History," or Mathematics" — articles written expressly with a female reader in mind. Toward the end of the eighteenth century, another periodical format appeared that reenvisioned the female reader. Exemplified by the *Lady's Magazine* and the *Lady's Monthly Museum*, these publications were designed to "blend entertainment and instruction in such a manner that they would suit 'the housewife as well as the peeress'" (quoted in White, 31).

The *Lady's Magazine* and *The Lady's Monthly Museum* contributed to the shaping of the modern British woman. While insisting that the maintenance of the household was a woman's primary responsibility, women's magazines also encouraged housewives to educate themselves in their spare time. Alongside articles about poetry and painting, the editors presented essays on "geography, chemistry, electricity, botany, animals and gardening" as well as a biyearly "Cabinet of Fashion" that included the first colored engravings to appear in a women's magazine (White, 28–33). Cynthia White summarizes these magazines as being "frank, vigorous and mentally stimulating, representing a cross-section of feminine (and often masculine) opinion, and reflecting a broad spectrum of interests and activities" (38). Beginning in the nineteenth century, however, there were "significant changes in the content and tone of women magazines [that was] consistent with a much narrower view of the role and status proper to women" (38).[20] Kathryn Shevelow writes that these new magazines "showed their gender-specificity through the absence as well as the presence of content, usually shunning 'masculine' public affairs in order to focus on 'feminine' private life" (152–53).

Unlike the British magazines discussed above, women's periodicals in the United States — such as *Woman's World*, *Women's Health and Beauty*, and *Ladies' Home Journal* — addressed themselves to lower- to middle-class housewives and unmarried working girls who worked in the shop or the factory and had little discretionary income to spend on personal and domestic items. The first Mexican magazines addressed to women, however, took their inspiration from the French and British examples and courted middle- to upper-class single and married women. *Godey's Lady's Book* was very popular in Mexican cities during the latter half of the nineteenth century, while Condé Nast's *Vogue*, the first illustrated fashion periodical published in the United States, was first published in Mexico in 1910. *La Mujer*, introduced to Mexican readers in 1880 by the School of Arts and Crafts for Women, promised to "educate women, disseminate useful ideas, about physiology and hygiene" (Ramos Escandón, 151 n. 22). In addition to articles on home economics, child care, and beauty culture, these Mexican publications assumed that their readers would also be interested in articles about current events, history, and philosophy.

La Mujer Mexicana (figure 4 above), was first published in 1904 and promoted as its goal "the physical, intellectual and moral improvement of women, the cultivation of sciences, fine arts and industry, the mutual assistance of the members of said society" (quoted in Tuñón Pablos, 81). In 1915 Señora Hermila Galindo, the editor of another women's

8. Señorita de
Palomeque,
a Mexican poetess,
La Mujer Moderna,
31 October 1915,
cover.

publication, *La Mujer Moderna* (figure 8), asserted that the primary
purpose of her weekly magazine was to "support Mexican women." To
this end, *La Mujer Moderna* included articles on the meaning of "elegance" and "beauty" as well as an essay outlining the many reasons why
women should be able to vote (3 October 1915). Galindo featured
essays concerned with social philosophy and national and international
news items in addition to articles on fashion, the arts, health, and home;
and *La Mujer Moderna* often graced its covers with photographs of Mexican women artists and writers. Finally, Mexican women also had access
to the most popular international fashion publications, such as *Vogue*, as
well to general women's magazines published in the United States, such
as *Ladies' Home Journal*.

As noted above, advertisements sell more than products and services. Advertising is based on the production and circulation of images that promote certain cultural ideals about the social world, about taste, about social status, and about "lifestyle." Advertisers in Mexico linked consumption to ideologies of middle-classness that included appeals to individualism, to particular conceptions of taste, to a politics of choice, and to an ideology of innovation as progress. In the 1920s and '30s, the products and technologies promoted as "modern" were visibly situated within a social tableau of what Roland Marchand calls "an ideal modern life" (176). Marchand adapted the phrase "social tableau" from the term "tableaux vivants" or "living pictures," which derived from a nineteenth-century genre of theater entertainment called *"tableaux vivants,"* meaning "staged representations of familiar scenes." According to Marchand, the entertainment value of these stagings "stemmed from the shock of recognition of a familiar scene suddenly 'brought to life' in three dimensions with real persons. The scenes, therefore, had to be familiar to the audience" (1985, 165).

In the same way, advertisements reproduced or "brought to life" familiar scenes for their readers. By familiar, I don't mean that audiences necessarily recognized themselves or their own lives in these modern tableaux; what they could apprehend, however, was a visible manifestation of a "modern life" which they could aspire to. An example of a modern "Mexican" life is presented in the tableaux vivants in figure 9, an advertisement in the illustrated magazine *El Tiempo Ilustrado* promoting El Palacio de Hiero, a popular department store in Mexico City. A group of obviously well-to-do, fashionable young women and their children enjoy afternoon tea in the store's café, a luxurious place that is decidedly feminized in its depiction of a gendered space absent of men. Yet, despite this seemingly conservative understanding of women's "place," the women depicted here are active: two seated at the table appear to be engaged in an animated conversation; their poses are self-assured instead of femininely timid. The standing woman in the foreground provides an object of identification for the readers of *El Tiempo Ilustrado*. Like her, the female readers are situated outside the frame of the tableaux vivants. After settling on her face, the reader's eye is drawn to the table of young mothers taking pleasure in each other's company as they enjoy a day of

Un detalle del natural, del "SALON TE" de
EL PALACIO DE HIERRO
MEXICO . . . . .

Gonciertos
los
MARTES
á las 4.30 p. m.

9. Afternoon tea at the Palacio de Hierro, *El Tiempo Ilustrado*,
28 January 1912, inside front cover.

leisure. Implicitly, they are asked to understand this woman's displeasure
at having to abandon the scene, perhaps to return home to prepare the
evening meal for the family. Even if they might not be able to afford the
dresses that adorn the models or attend afternoon tea at El Palacio de
Hiero, modern female readers could understand the tension between
pleasure and responsibility, between the freedom to window-shop and
converse with friends in public versus the duty of the wife and mother in
the private space of the home.

The motion picture theater was another venue that modeled modernity for its audiences. The arrival of motion pictures in Mexico, perhaps more than any other contemporary invention, brought modernity
into the lives of both urban and rural Mexicans. Representatives of the
Lumières, manufacturers of film equipment, introduced cinema to Mexico City audiences on 14 August 1896 in the Plateros Pharmacy with
eight short films, including *Arrival of a Train*, *The Groundskeeper*, and *The
Gardener and the Boy*. As in Paris and New York, audiences were shocked,

astonished, amazed, and, most of all, curious. One of the first film reviews published in Mexico, by Luis G. Urbina in *El Universal* on 23 August 1896, confirms the public's fascination with the new diversion: "What a wonderful way to enjoy oneself! There, inside, is China with its houses of strange turrets[,] . . . over there is the temple of Buddha with his paunchy stomach[,] . . . there is Egypt with its plains of dry yellow earth and its burning sky" (Quoted in González Casanova, 79).

Mexicans soon had the opportunity to see themselves on the screen as well as French, Chinese, and Egyptians. The U.S. film equipment manufacturer Edison and the Lumière company dispatched emissaries to Mexico to film local events and subjects in Mexico. At the same time, Mexican entrepreneurs were buying the Lumière Cinématographes (which functioned as a camera, projector, and film printer), and shooting their own short films. They set out to experiment with the new technology of moving pictures, capturing scenes of everyday life in Mexico. As the filmmakers perfected their techniques, the short two- or three-minute "vistas" became documents about important national events and the daily public life of the nation and its peoples, fiestas and catastrophes, social and political events.

If Mexico's first filmmakers came from the educated middle and upper classes of Mexico, the audience was primarily composed of the new urban proletariat that was, for the most, part illiterate. While many in the moneyed and intellectual sectors of society condemned the cinema, the cheap price of entertainment and the promise that one did not have to be literate to enjoy the films drew the lower classes into motion picture venues. The cinema, in other words, democratized popular entertainment and offered its audiences pictures and narratives of other ways of living that had not been available before the advent of motion pictures. Previously, European and American literature and theater had only been within reach of a privileged literate, educated, and wealthy segment of the population. Now, Mexicans of all social and economic classes had access to a truly transnational mode of communication.

As pointed out in the beginning of this chapter, the Mexican film *Santa* repeatedly employs the female body to visualize modernity. In addition to the introductory scene discussed earlier, there are numerous references to this body. The opening shot in a scene that occurs midway through the film features a close-up of an RCA Victor radio that is play-ing a popular song by the well-known composer Agustín Lara. (This scene was not included in Gamboa's 1903 novel, as radio was not yet part of Mexican daily life.) The camera dollies back to reveal Santa dancing to the song in her bedroom. Hipólito, the blind piano player who enter-tains the girls of the brothel and their customers, enters the room and waits for the music to finish. While the scene does contribute to the narrative's imperative — it demonstrates Hipólito's love for the beautiful and unattainable Santa — it functions primarily to showcase the new technology of sound by making a radio and its music the central charac-ter of the scene. What is most interesting, however, is the way in which the scene explicitly links the body of modern technology — the radio — to Santa's body. As the song plays, the scene cuts back and forth between the radio and Santa as they "perform" for the camera. The blind Hipólito can't see Santa; both the radio and Santa's performances are addressed to the cinema audience. They are presented not as distinct entities but as different manifestations or parts of a larger social construction — that of modernity.

Although I have attempted to paint a picture of a particular historical moment in Mexican history in order to contextualize the emergence of la chica moderna, history cannot be so easily organized. History is messy, multivalent, and filled with contradictions; it is not linear and thus has no definitive beginnings or endings. The period I am defining by cir-cumscribing it between the years 1917 and 1940 is best described as a convulsive moment marked by rapidly changing social, economic, and cultural conditions brought on by a protracted civil war known as the Mexican revolution. While all signifiers are mobile, in moments like these, they are radically so as various historical institutions and actors vie for political, economic, and cultural dominance. In regards to woman, the major conflict during this period involved the structural antagonisms between Mexican patriarchy and Mexican capitalism, each of which posed demands on women that were often in conflict with each other. At the same time, the intersection of these two institutions redefined cul-tural meanings of femininity, female sexuality, and female social and national identities.

Chapter 2

En México como en París:

Fashioning *la Chica Moderna*

One of the transnational discourses that shaped *la chica moderna* was that of fashion (figure 10 below). Fashion is often dismissed as peripheral and unimportant, while women's concern with fashion is seen as simply a product or effect of consumerist ideology. Fashion, however, serves more than a functional, decorative, or commercial purpose; it is a practice through which one constructs and presents a "bodily self," a visible identity (Craik, 1). In the 1920s and '30s, Mexican women eagerly perused newspapers and magazines for information on how to dress and act like a modern woman. Articles and advertisements in the popular press advised women on what to wear for particular occasions, how to apply their makeup, and how to keep their figure trim and healthy, while mass-produced, ready-to-wear fashions and mass-produced images helped shape their own sense of identity. The visual representations

fears and anxieties about modern fashion

of fashion in advertisements and in beauty articles carried in the pages of magazines and newspapers emphasized the modern notion that appearance was central to women's identity and that identity could be changed through physical self-transformation and the consumption of commodities. This "revolution" in fashion's function can be connected to significant social and economic changes, including the rise of a consumer culture across an emerging middle class, the accelerated movement of more and more women into the workforce and other public spaces, and what Kathy Peiss calls the "changing cultural perceptions of the relationship between women's identity and appearance" as what one looked like and what one wore came to be identified as a reflection of who one "was" (1996, 312).

In Mexico, as in many other parts of the world, public discussions about gender often centered on the realm of women's fashion, provoking heated debates that condemned and celebrated the modern woman's appearance. Cultural critics interpreted modern fashion and women's concern with fashion as evidence of dangerous foreign influence, widespread moral decline, and a particularly visible indication of a feminist emancipation. Some commentators pointed to women's preoccupation with fashion as indicative of moral decadence; others saw it as a dangerous sign of modernity's obsession with conspicuous consumption; Catholics and other conservatives argued that participating in the sphere of fashion led women down a perilous, immoral path.

opposed

An editorial in *El Tepeyac*, a magazine for women published by the Catholic Church, for example, ranted against those foreigners who "imposed fashion" on susceptible moral Christian women. According to the writer, women who fell prey to the lure of these new "indecorous styles . . . were victims of foreign fashionistas who exerted a humiliating tyranny over all who accept their fashion designs." It was not just particular fashion styles that offended this writer; he was also concerned with the fact that women who were "tyrannized" by fashion were forced to visit department stores which were dangerous places populated by unscrupulous people "of both sexes who distain with 'rancidity' and 'fanaticisms' ancient habits of honesty" (July 1926, 3–4). Another writer in the popular weekly publication *Jueves de Excelsior* laments the fact

10. "In Mexico as in Paris," *Revista de Revistas*, 18 May 1924, 33.

that although young Mexican women may be reluctant to "obey the proclamations of the couturiers," they have "taken themselves to the hairdresser to have their beautiful hair cut off." While he personally believes that short hair is "unfeminine," the writer does not see the bobbing of one's hair as a symbol of lax morals, or a conscious rebellion, or a "heroic sacrifice." Instead, he dismisses it as merely a simple impulse to follow a fashion imposed on one country by another (24 April 1924).

Conversely, some journalists celebrated fashion as an arena through which women could assert their new-found autonomy and independence. An article in "La página femenina" (the women's page) in a 1920 issue of *El Heraldo Ilustrado* emphasizes women's freedom to choose among a variety of fashion options. The article proclaims the democratic nature of fashion, asserting that "the adaptability of today's fashion starts precisely from the ready-made fact of its capriciousness and rebelliousness in all of its manifestations." Photographs of real women reproduced in the society pages of Sunday supplements and weekly magazines disclose that Mexican women of the middle class enthusiastically adopted modern fashions as expressions of their own changing lives.

Fashion also played a part in the debates around an emerging, post-revolutionary feminism.[1] Some cartoons portrayed feminists as unfashionable. Others commented on the centrality of fashion in all aspects of a modern woman's life. An eight-panel *historieta* (comic book) entitled "El día de una torera" (A Woman Bullfighter's Day) published in 1898 in *El Hijo del Ahuizote*, chronicles the busy workday of a female bullfighter. The strip, described by Juan Manuel Aurrecoechea and Armando Bartra as "a protofeminist comic" depicts the bullfighter at seven in the morning feeding her baby (who looks suspiciously like a small husband), going to the marketplace to shop, dressing for the bullfight, fighting the bull, and finally, at eight in the evening, preparing tamales for her baby/husband (82). Fashion functions centrally in each of the eight panels that make up this historieta. *La torera* wears different clothes for each of her roles, and each outfit is gendered: she wears a dress for cooking and shopping but dons the traditional male torero outfit for her job, battling the bull. The baby/husband, conversely, is pictured in the three panels in an undistinguished night shirt.

A political cartoon on the front page of a 1925 edition of *Excelsior*, entitled "En pleno feminismo," or "at the height of feminism," obviously a play on the phrase "at the height of fashion," ridicules a number of feminist "types" who are defined primarily by their hats and their obvious unattractiveness (figure 11 shows a similar satirical piece). One of these feminists sports a bowl-shaped hat and a mustache, while the berries decorating another's hat matched similarly shaped warts that adorned her nose; a woman's black hat matched her sunglasses and her black teeth (12 July 1925, 1). The weekly illustrated magazine, *Revista de Revista*, uses the same caricature to remind its female audience "not to forget to buy our 'Feminist Edition,' the issue that all women must read."

11. Caricatures of contemporary fashion, *El Heraldo Ilustrado*, 30 May 1920, unpaginated.

12. An example of a modern young ladies' fashion, *El Tiempo Ilustrado*, 9 April 1905, unpaginated.

Modelo de abrigo de terciopelo.

Why did seemingly trivial matters like dress style or length of hair provoke such heated political discussions? What did it matter to society in general if young girls bobbed their hair and wore the latest Paris fashions or spent their afternoons shopping at downtown department stores? How and why did feminism get dragged into the fashion debate? In this chapter, I examine pictures of fashionable women in the women's pages of newspapers and magazines, as central to advertising campaigns, and as represented in motion pictures in order to explore the ways in which fashion and discussions about fashion participated in the making of la chica moderna. Because fashion is a strikingly visual symbol of change and of sexuality, it is a rich site through which to explore cultural understandings of social transformation. While dress style did circumscribe modern life by confirming dominant notions of gender, sexuality, and class, modern fashion's democratic nature provided a space in which women could cultivate practices of agency and self-determination in the context of their everyday personal and public lives.

In the realm of fashion, clothing participates in the narrative of individual and social identity through its symbolic and expressive capacities. Dress, argues Mary Louise Roberts, "has an "eloquence of its own" (1993, 662–65). Another way of putting it is that fashion is communicative; it speaks to and about culture, about individual taste and character traits (figure 12, above). At the same time, the wearing of particular clothes is more than a social or psychological "fashion statement." While fashion does impart meaning, it cannot be compared to speech acts or declarations because fashion is, above all, visible and therefore appeals directly to our sense of sight through our engagement with drawings and photographs of fashionable women.

The first popular visions of fashion can be found in fashion illustration that emerged in the eighteenth century, primarily in France and Great Britain, as a practice distinct from though related to fine art. In contrast to illustrations that featured clothed figures, fashion drawings were intended to illustrate "actual clothing" or to foreground the idealized dressed body (Hollander, 317–27). Commercial fashion plates produced expressly for promoting fashion appeared in European women's magazines by the middle of the nineteenth century. These images,

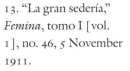

13. "La gran sedería," *Femina*, tomo I [vol. 1], no. 46, 5 November 1911.

first drafted for publication in watercolor, then reproduced as engravings and later as color lithographs, often pictured two or more women modeling dress fashions, generally situated in the context of the private venue of the home or a public location such as the park or a theater (Marcus, 10).

Fashion plates were addressed to women and structured for the female gaze; male figures were rarely included. In many of the ads, such as the one pictured in figure 13 (above), one of the women in the composition is pictured observing another woman or group of women. Sharon Marcus describes this structure of looking "in which women consume images of women" as homoerotic (12). By homoerotic, Marcus is not suggesting a structure of desire or of "lesbian looking relations." In the context of the nineteenth century, for example, "homoeroticism encompassed companionship, love, caretaking, self-sacrifice, admiration, longing, obsession, physical intimacy, and intense excitement and passion — all also crucial components of heteroeroticism" (6). Marcus's point is that attraction between women may be seen as a relation that includes sexual desire *for* or identification *with* the other woman, but also encompasses other kinds of desire such as the longing to *be* or *be like* the other. At the turn of the century, fashion advertisements adapted the aesthetics and formal structures of the fashion plates to re-create this "erotics of looking" for modern consumers. Female figures modeling the newest fashions offered women an object of identification through which they might imagine themselves in the guise of the model.

Initially, women's magazines carried very few advertisements; the ads generally appeared on the back pages of the publications and did not include any images. The last page of an early 1905 edition of *El Tiempo Ilustrado* featured text ads for a new housing development in Mexico City's exclusive Colonia Roma, an elixir that promised to prevent monthly menstrual bleeding, and a "marvelous" new hair pomade. By 1910, most magazines were carrying advertisements that included some kind of illustration. Fashion advertisements in the form of engravings were interspersed among articles that addressed housekeeping as well as beauty and health issues. A 1911 edition of *Femina* featured an ad for a store called La Gran Sedería that announced the newest fashion, "a great variety of white blouses." The ad also included engravings of two "Traje Princesa" dresses that were available for purchase: "No. 9928" and "No. 9925." The ad was placed next to a column that featured recipes for the housewife (1 February 1911, no page). Five years later, La Gran Sedería was still in business. An ad in the same magazine announced a "grand winter exhibition" of recent arrivals from the major European and American fashion centers, and ran alongside an article entitled "Mujer inexperta" (*Femina*, 5 November 1916, no. 46, no page). A 1912 edition of *El Tiempo Ilustrado*, featured a hand-drawn lithograph promoting one of the major department stores in Mexico City, El Centro Mercantile, and announced the availability of the "newest dress fashion."

Advertisements addressed to women in the national daily newspapers, such as *Excelsior*, or weekly illustrated magazines like *El Heraldo Ilustrado* and *El Tiempo Ilustrado*, were most often found in the "women's section" of the dailies, situated next to columns that spoke to topics concerned with fashion, beauty regimes, and domesticity. The 8 August 1920 issue of *El Heraldo Ilustrado* celebrated a "new format and printing process" with its "Página Femenina" (women's page). A sixteen-page, 1 December 1916 issue of *El Hogar*, a publication that promoted itself as "the family magazine," also featured a section entitled "Páginas Femininas," which included an article on woolen hats and three ads — one for a new electric tamale maker, another for a dressmaker who specialized in formal dresses and foreign fashions, and a women's clothing shop that featured "simple and elegant lounging pajamas."

By the 1920s, the most visible venues for modern fashion were the women's sections of newspapers, and those women's magazines that conceptualized fashion as central to modern lives. Articles advised women on what to wear for particular occasions, how to apply their makeup, and how to keep their figure trim and healthy while at the same time advocating ways of being modern. For example "La página femenina" in a 1920 issue of *El Heraldo Ilustrado* (figure 14) advises its readers that "the best styles of this season are blouses that drape over the skirt and carefully crafted skirts made of distinctive materials." Women also learn that "today, ribbons are obligatory companions for women who wish to dress elegantly and economically." More important, however, drawings and photographs of women dressed in the latest fashion styles from Paris and New York, modeled how to be modern. It was not just the clothes these models wore that defined them as modern; it was their hairstyle, their body type and the way they held their bodies, the expressions on their faces, and the social milieus in which they appeared.

Compare the women in the ad for Lydia E. Pinkham's Compuesto Vegetal, a popular "health tonic" (figure 15) with the photographs of "Mujeres bonitas de Colima" (Beautiful women from Colima; figure 16). In the Pinkham advertisement, five tall, slim cosmopolitan women model similarly up-to-date fashions in a contemporary public space in which men and women mingle freely. Nothing in the tableau identifies the setting as "Mexico"; the scene could be staged in any modern city —

Pagina femenina

Por L. Fortuño

En la temporada actual son de gran moda las blusas que caen sobre la falda, y las confeccionadas de telas distintas a las de las faldas. Tiene esto la ventaja de que se preste a numerosas combinaciones. Pueden esas blusas acompañar a una falda más o menos complicada, y si no, se escogen colores que contrasten. Si la blusa es de color de porcelana, podría acompañar una falda de color delicado de canela. Además, esas blusas se prestan para usarlas con traje de sastre, o con una falda de tafeta. Las blusas se confeccionan en telas ligeras, crepé, georgette, sedas suaves, de batista, etc., etc., admiten todas las fantasías en clase de adornos.

Las flores de organdí sean blancas o de color, confeccionadas a mano, pueden colocarse como adorno, sean solas o formando bellas guirnaldas en corpiños de trajes de noche, o en el ala de un sombrero, o en nuestros otro adorno para completar su espiritualidad. Ningún traje conviene mejor a una jovencita, que uno blanco, fresco, vaporoso, terminado con un encantador fichú.

En nuestros días las cintas son las obli-

gadas compañeras de las mujeres que desean vestirse con elegancia y economía. Se confeccionan con ellas corpiños, vestidos, así como cinturones, escogiéndolos de tintes vivos, de colores radiantes, que producen espléndidos efectos.

La adaptabilidad de la moda actual, arranca precisamente del hecho de ser caprichosa y rebelde en todas sus manifestaciones. Puesto que la moda ha venido patrocinando una extensa variedad de siluetas, y modifica las líneas esbeltas de las últimas temporadas con las alforzas, los efectos abollonados de 1830, el tontillo de 1885, los drapeados en las caderas y las líneas rectas del llamado estilo egipcio, las señoras pueden escoger libremente lo que más las favorezca. A medida que avanza el verano, vemos cada vez más marcada la tendencia a emplear la mayor variedad de adornos. Porque es claro que los encajes, las tabletas, los bordados y las flores, que tanto se utilizan ahora como adornos de sombreros, de trajes y abrigos en general, le imparten un sello de renovada elegancia a las prendas de precios moderados. Como que para efectuar la transformación de cualquier traje

bastará adornarlo con una banda de cinta, por ejemplo, o con tiras de organdí o batista, en la cintura, o bien darle un osado toque de color, en la forma de una guirnalda de flores. Los sombreros también se prestan a ese proceso de renovación, y aun cuando a menudo se confeccionan éstos de tafetas, raso, tul, encaje y organdí, solos o combinados con pajas, no faltan algunos, encantadoramente originales, de guinga, o de esos estampados ingleses, para no decir nada de los de cerda, paja de Milán, paja tagala, y paja liseré, naturalmente más costosos.

Aunque en otro sentido, la popularidad de los encajes favorece también a la causa de la economía, ya que París ha decidido acordarle su suprema sanción a sombreros cuyo chic y cuya gracia dependen de los velos graciosamente drapeados, que constituyen su único adorno. De donde resulta que los velos de encaje, tanto el punto, y los de malla, están muy en voga para acompañar a los sombreros de todas clases, formas y tamaños.

Los peinados varían de forma, según la moda; los actuales son fáciles de llevar, pues sólo requieren un moño flojo más o menos bajo.

La ondulación aumenta el volumen del cabello. Esta persiste, según la naturaleza del pelo, unas horas o varias semanas, si se emplea la ondulación Marcel, que imita tan bien las ondas naturales. En todo tiempo las mujeres han recurrido a la on-

cabellera. Las griegas se ondulaban por medio de fierros calientes, las romanas, entrenzándose el pelo. Los predicadores en la Edad Media batallaban contra las ondas lujuriosas de la cabellera, lo que prueba que la cabellera lisa no era una generalidad. Las coquetas del Renacimien-

to llevaban unas mechas onduladas, las del tiempo de Luis XIII "orejas de perro" y ricitos en la frente. Son raras las épocas en que los cabellos lisos han sido de moda. Ahora todavía, en que la ondulación está admitida por casi todas las mujeres. Algunas quisieran usar la cabellera lisa, pero es muy difícil que la adopten las señoras que siguen la moda.

¿La ondulación con fierro caliente es acaso nociva al pelo? Generalmente si está bien hecha con un fierro moderadamente caliente, no tiene grandes inconvenientes. Algunos creen que el color impide las canas, por lo mismo está demostrado que puede usarse la ondulación artificial, con moderación.

Una de nuestras lectoras nos pregunta cuáles son los abrigos que más se llevan este verano. La capa es la triunfante. Las mismas formas que se vieron en el último invierno se repiten en telas ligeras, los matices son claros, pero las líneas generales son las mismas.

Para las capas de verano se escogen tafetas negras, bronceadas, rasos azul marino, o marrón, crespones de China, crespones georgette, que son las telas encantadoras que emplea la moda actual. Se hacen igualmente capas cortas a cuadros o con rayas semejantes al traje que acompañan, a menos que sean totalmente distintas. Para excursiones, viajes y días de campo, las largas capas escocesas son utilísimas y encantadoras. Para de noche se usan elegantísimas capas de raso o crespón de China bordadas de oro, de perlas, o de rafia. Se adornan también con gruesas escarolas de tafeta o de tul, estas últimas comienzan a ser de gran moda.

14. "The Woman's Page" with fashion advice for all the ladies, *El Heraldo Ilustrado*, 8 August 1920, unpaginated.

En todas las sendas de la vida. . .

Compre este paquete. Rechace toda imitación

LA SALUD es el secreto de la felicidad.

La vida no vale la pena de vivirse, ni con todo el dinero del mundo, si está uno enferma o débil.

El Compuesto Vegetal de Lydia E. Pinkham hace que desaparezcan todos los do-

irregularidad de la menstruación y los dolores consiguientes.

Destierra las jaquecas mensuales. Quedan olvidados los dolores de la parte baja del cuerpo y de la espalda y se logra realmente la alegría de vivir tomado regular y fielmente el Compuesto de Lydia E. Pinkham.

Hace cincuenta años que el Compuesto de Lydia E. Pinkham viene

15. A tableau of fashionable, modern women, out in public, *Revista de Revistas*, 18 May 1924, 21.

Buenos Aires, Berlin, New York, São Paulo. The women are relaxed in their poses; a few carry an armload of books, indicating that they're educated and well read. The woman in the right-hand side of the frame strikes a self-assured stance, one hand on her hip, her body thrust confidently forward.

Conversely, "Las mujeres bonitas" featured in a 1914 issue of *La Semana Ilustrado* are not wearing dresses illustrative of modern femininity as understood by the majority of Mexican women consumers. Their dress styles, long hair, and head coverings are markedly old-fashioned,

Mujeres bonitas de Colima

16. "Beautiful women of Colima," *La Semana Ilustrado*, 27 January 1914, unpaginated.

signifying "costumes" rather than fashion. "Las mujeres de Colima" don't share the slim silhouettes of la chica moderna, and whereas the women in the Pinkham ad appear to be relaxed and unaware of the viewer's gaze, the formal postures and direct gaze of Indian women appear stiff and apprehensive. Finally, the studio setting denotes a private, concealed place associated with traditional notions of feminine space instead of the public space now available to la chica moderna.

The Transnational Space of Fashion

Historians point to the effects the First World War had on fashion design, the fashion industry, and the democratization of fashion around the world, bringing about "significant changes in fashion design, dress fabrics, and methods of clothing manufacture" as well as in fashion promotion (Mendes and de la Haye, 48–51). The industrialization of the textile and clothing industries introduced not only mechanized tools of production, but also new manufacturing modes defined by mass production or "fordism."[2] The industries that promoted modern fashion to women were, by the early twentieth century, global in their reach. The introduction and marketing of dress patterns, the accessibility of less expensive synthetic materials, the appearance of department stores in large and small urban centers, and the increased representation of fashion in women's magazines and in the cinema, put Paris and New York fashion styles in the hands of modern, middle-class women all over the world, offering ordinary women fashionable glamour and economical alternatives to haute couture.

This explosion of fashion coincided with the rise of advertising specifically addressed to women and with the emergence of an imaginary "female space" concerned with beauty and fashion (Peiss 1998, 166). In Mexico City—as in London, Paris, New York, and Des Moines—advertisers marketed the same "ready-to-wear" styles that were presented as "fashionable" all over the world. International fashion publications such as *Vogue*, as well Mexican magazines catering to women, took part in the promotion of women's fashion as well as new ways to be a woman. While Paris was the center of the new "fashion system," this system was not just for Parisians. The biggest market for ready-to-wear clothes was, in fact, in Asia, India, and Latin America (Mendes and de la Haye, 80–81). Although, Paris remained the center of fashion design into the twentieth century, in the United States "ready-to-wear clothing displaced made-to-order clothing almost entirely" (138). By 1930, America led the world in the mass production of clothing in standardized sizes.

At the turn of the century the fashionable modern woman was exemplified by a number of primary "types" that exhibited, to differing degrees, various traits of modernity and traditional femininity. The feminine woman gained fame in the first decade of the new century through the popular pen-and-ink drawings of the "Gibson Girl," pictured in figure 12 above. Created by Charles Dana Gibson for the cover of *Life Magazine*, the Gibson Girl dresses in a shirtwaist that falls to her ankles and boasts a small bustle; she wears her hair piled into a chignon that is topped by a jaunty hat; she is the epitome of a conventional yet at the same time modern femininity. In spite of her hairstyle and ankle-length dress, she is often pictured holding a golf club or tennis racket.[3] American illustrators such as Ethel Plummer (1888–1936) and Rita Senger (active 1915–1930s), whose work was commissioned for the covers and stories of upscale magazines such as *Vogue* and *Vanity Fair*, updated the Gibson Girl by incorporating European modernist aesthetics, placing her in public urban settings, and rendering her as not only fashionable, but also poised and confident (Kitch, 12). "La muchacha Gibson" looked just like her Euro-American sisters and modeled the "latest dress styles" available at grand department stores in Mexico City such as La Gran Sedería and El Centro Mercantil.

At the end of World War I Paris fashion "followed two courses — the traditionally feminine look," and the more modernist or *garçonne* look that was described as simple, youthful, boyish, and "sleek" and indicated a young woman who was independent and progressive, bobbed her hair, and unashamedly wore makeup. Although styles were simple, fabrics "were highly decorative," borrowing from the past and from "exotic" cultures that included Slavic, Egyptian, Indian, and Chinese influences. After the 1925 Exposition Internationale des Arts Décoratifs et Industriels Modernes in Paris, "the smooth, angular and geometric lines of modernism soon dominated both fashion and textile design." In Europe and the United States, hemlines were shortened, styles became less decorative and more casual and practical (Mendes and de la Haye, 55–66).

The modernist look of fashion that ultimately took over in the 1920s was further emphasized by the modern "stances, silhouettes, and accessories" of "the Fisher Body girl" who was "slender, youthful, and sophisticated," and the "high-fashion" silhouette exemplified by Art Deco figures (figure 17). Marchand notes that these "types" functioned to

17. Art Deco
and international
femininity,
Mujer Moderna,
31 October 1915,
inside front
cover.

differentiate social class: for example, the woman of high social status
is pictured as nine feet tall with an exaggerated neck, elongated feet
and hands, and a "Grecian" profile (Marchand, 179–82). In France,
another female type, the garçonne, was famously publicized by French
fashion designers such as Paul Poiret, who is credited among other
things with doing away with the corset, and Gabrielle "Coco" Chanel
(1883–1971).[4] Chanel insisted that she was committed to making fashions "women can live in, breath in, feel comfortable in and look younger
in" (quoted in Ewing, 100).

The French garçonne became the "flapper" in Britain and the United
States, and *la flapperista* (sometimes referred to as *la flaperesca*) in Mexico (figure 18). She enacted the idea of a modern woman as well as a
lifestyle made available to those who could afford to buy the trappings of

that life: the clothes, the cosmetics, the middle-class household furnishings. She was neither a wife nor a mother; she was young and active and independent. The American illustrator, John Held, is often credited with popularizing the visual iconography of the American version of the "flapper" on the pages of publications as diverse as the *New Yorker*, *Ladies' Home Journal*, *Life*, *Good Housekeeping*, and *Harper's Bazaar* in the 1920s. In an essay in the *New Republic* Bruce Bliven describes the flapper as "very pretty. . . . [She is] heavily made-up. . . . [She has] pallor mortis, poisonously scarlet lips, richly ringed eyes." But it was her clothes that most intrigued Bliven: he describes her underwear as "exceedingly brief but roomy"; her dress "is also brief. It is cut low where it might be high, and vice versa. The skirt comes just an inch below her knees, overlapping by a faint fraction her rolled and twisted stockings"; and, finally, he remarks on the fact that her "haircut is also abbreviated" (9 September 1925). Advertisers and magazine publishers quickly realized the marketing potential of these female types that appealed to the modern taste of educated, urban, young women.[5] The flapperista sold fashion, cigarettes, and hand cream. But, most important, she marketed a particular kind of modern femininity associated with rebellion, controversy, self-determination, and independence.

The flapperista enjoyed the same notoriety in Mexico: she was never pictured at home but was the talk of the town in the popular press. While some vilified her as *una malinchista*, subject to the influence of the United States and thus a traitor, many celebrated her youthful vibrancy and sense of fashion. A cigarette hanging from her mouth, eyes ringed in dark makeup, her direct and unflinching, immodest gaze at the viewer, her bobbed hair, and, most of all, her unconcealed sexuality exemplified either everything wrong with modernity's challenge to conventional gender roles or everything right to those who celebrated women's emerging independence. Celebrities from the theater and cinema modeled the flapper fashion in advertisements and on the social pages of the national media. Lupe Vélez, the beautiful young movie star who had become successful in Hollywood posed in a 1926 issue of *Revista de Revista* as an "ultramodern" flapperista (figure 19). She was the quintessential transnational symbol of the modern: a familiar local figure in the guise of an exotic global icon.

18. La flapperista, *Revista de Revista*, 25 May 1924, front cover.

 upe Vélez, la tiple-radio, en una pose ultra-moderna.

os personajes estrechamente uni-
os por un bigote. Al fin, el peque-
o cedió y abandonó su presa. El
eñor Balbís aprovechó aquel ins-
ante para separarle un poco, y le
airó, temeroso de otro ataque. Pe-

19. "Lupe Vélez, the radio soprano in an ultra-modern 'pose,'" *Revista de Revista*, 7 February 1926, 31.

As indicated above, fashion is more than just style of dress; fashion offers women new ways to be. One of the most prolific meanings associated with modern fashion "was" that of independence and freedom from spaces and activities associated with traditional understandings of femininity. For example, fashion images were rarely situated in the home kitchen or in the workplace. As we will see in chapter 3, advertisements that did picture fashionable women engaged in household chores were selling new ovens or miracle cleansers, not the newest Paris fashion. One modern activity that fashionable women did take up was cigarette smoking. Up until the end of World War I, there was a general social stigma against women smoking in public, although this did not stop women from lighting up. The only women pictured smoking in eighteenth- and nineteenth-century illustrations were prostitutes. Despite a continued critique of smoking as "immoral," the practice became more widespread around the world after the war and general attitudes toward it shifted. More women were smoking in public in defiance of outright social and legal bans. Recognizing this shift, the tobacco industry began to specifically target women by utilizing "ideas of liberty and power" and, at the same time, attempting to "overcome the association with louche and libidinous behavior" (Amos and Hagalund, 3). A full-page advertisement for Monte Carlo cigarettes, for example, features two young women wearing hats cocked jauntily over their bobbed cuts, holding cigarettes in their hands as if smoking was the most natural thing in the world. The ad informs its readers that "naturally, charming and interesting women smoke Monte Carlo" (*Todo*, 19 March 1935).

The American and European tobacco industry began to advertise directly to women in the 1920s. Philip Morris designed the Marlboro brand for women, positioning it through package design and advertising "as a premium-priced smoke for women" that is as "Mild as May" (Kluger, 74). The original ad for this campaign featured an elegantly dressed woman, with a fashionable bob and a string of pearls, relaxing on a chaise lounge and holding a cigarette. The text tells us that "Women — when they smoke at all — quickly develop discerning taste. This is why Marlboros reside in so many limousines, attend so many bridge parties, repose in so many handbags."[6] An ad campaign for Lucky Strike, launched by the American Tobacco Company in 1928, invited women to

20. "Favorita, a cigarette made especially for women," *Excelsior*, 18 March 1924, unpaginated.

"Reach for Lucky instead of a sweet," promising that cigarette smoking would help to control weight. In 1923, women consumed only 5 percent of all cigarettes sold. By 1929, the number had grown to 12 percent, and it jumped to 18.1 percent by 1933 (O'Keefe and Pollay, 67–69). Lucky Strike also mounted an appeal to first-wave feminism, promoting cigarettes as "torches of freedom." Cigarette advertising in Mexico was modeled on American and European promotional campaigns for smoking.[7] Mexican cigarette companies, such as El Buen Tono, Claveles, and La Cigarrera Mexicana, developed ad campaigns that pictured modern women who smoked. The Mexican-made cigarette Favorita, one of the brands produced by Cigarrera Mexicana, was made specifically for and marketed to women. Favorita's packaging featured the image of an attractive, fashionable, and modern woman promoting Favorita and another Mexican cigarette, Modernista (figure 20).

In addition to smoking, modern women also drove cars. Stories of women "in the driver's seat" emerged when cars were introduced at the end of the nineteenth century, although driving was initially considered a masculine practice. Automobile advertising increased dramatically in popular magazines between 1904 and 1910 and was generally aimed at upper- or middle-class men, calling attention to such attributes as "dependability." Julie Wosk finds advertising images of women drivers as early as 1899 although these early images tended to be used to add "decorative and sexual allure to magazine covers and posters for automobile shows." She notes however, that "by the 1920s, photographs of women and automobiles had also become a central cultural emblem of women's modernity, independence and mobility" and female celebrities were regularly featured in the driver's seat as car manufacturers sought to expand their markets (118–20). However, the ads were most often clearly gendered. Wosk describes an automobile advertisement in *Vogue*, for example, that marketed a Lexington auto as "'a man's car in power and speed' and 'a woman's car because of its luxury, ease of handling, and simplicity of control'" (133–34). Pictures of women in the driver's seat, however, also "sold" the idea that driving was something that modern woman could do. A *Revista de Revista* article presents three photographs of female drivers. In one, a group of young friends are "crewing" an automobile; in another, a well-dressed "female chauffer is at the wheel of her car"; a third photograph reveals another young woman "ready for the road" (figure 21).

Fashion and Film

Wide shoulders and slender hips seemed to be every woman's
ideal, exemplified in the figure of Greta Garbo.
—LAVER, *Costume and Fashion: A Concise History*, 244

Mexican theater stars had long been featured in the Mexican press. *La Vida Moderna: Semanario Ilustrado* often pictured popular theater actresses on its front cover. Dor Martínez Siliceo, the "first young lady of the Teatro Alarcón," for example, graced the cover of the 9 November 1916 issue. "La popular 'Mayita,'" or Margarita Carvajal, who debuted with "great" success in the Teatro Lírico, was featured in a regular column

Un grupo de simpáticas damitas, tripulando un automóvil.

Una guapísima "chauffeuse", en el volante de su carro.

Dispuesta para el paseo...

21. Mexican women: "Ready for the road," *Revista de Revista*, 29 June 1924, 9.

about theater in Mexico City in the weekly *Ilustrado* (4 April 1929, 11) wearing one of her costumes. However, theater actresses always appeared in the context of the theater pages, promoting particular plays or theatrical companies. Rarely did the stories address these actresses as "real" women or tell stories about their private lives.

With the rising popularity of the cinema, international motion picture actresses became exemplars of modern femininity for Mexican women. The Italian film actress Pina Mcnichelli is credited with introducing the concept of the motion picture "star" or "diva" to Mexican film audiences. In the role of a depraved modern woman in the 1915 Italian film, *Il Fuoco* (directed by Giovanni Pastrone), the story of a doomed affair between a poor artist and a wealthy woman, Menichelli established the femme fatale as a cinematic female stereotype and in doing so also provided an "appearance" that women could imitate. While European stars ruled the first decade of film culture in Mexico, by the 1920s the Hollywood movie star was the girl to emulate.

Hollywood movie stars embodied the dominant, transnational standards of modern beauty promoted by the international fashion and cosmetic markets and were utilized extensively to advance various ideologies of modernity and the modern woman to American and international audiences. By 1925, Hollywood movie stars had emerged as profitable commodities or "sites of productivity" (de Cordova, 19).[8] Stars were used to differentiate a studio's product from the products of other studios and to distinguish one motion picture from another. Stars also served as markers of standardization in that films could be promoted as a "Mary Pickford" film or a film starring Clark Gable or Douglas Fairbanks. And around the world, Hollywood movie stars were setting the fashion for style and beauty through the marketing of the stars themselves and through product tie-ins. Young Hollywood starlets such as Clara Bow and Colleen Moore served as fashion role models for women all over the world.

In Mexico, newspaper advertisements, film posters, and public appearances by directors and movie stars, as well as public gossip and discussions about films and stars, used images of stars to promote films, fashion, cosmetics, and lifestyles. An article in the Sunday supplement of *El Diario del Sureste*, the major daily newspaper in the Yucatán city of

22. The popularity of Hollywood stars in Mexico, "Con las estrellas," *Sucesos para Todos*, 12 April 1933, 62.

23. At home with Betty Grable, *Hoy*, 24 April 1937, 40.

Mérida, suggested that women "who pursue glamour, are at times able to succeed in their quest by copying the individual details of the fashion of some movie stars, such as the hairstyle of Carole Lombard, for example" (13 February 1938).

Women borrowed not just fashion *styles* from the movies and from their favorite stars; they also envisioned themselves as acting out the screen parts of their favorite female stars or sharing a history of studying ballet with Eleanor Powell (figure 22, above). A photograph of Betty Grable appearing in an article entitled "Como viven las estrellas" (How the Stars Live) (figure 23, above) in the weekly magazine *Hoy* offers Mexican women not only a particular "at home" fashion image and ideas about home decorating, but also "ways to be" and ways to dress at home. The idea of "home" was envisioned as more than just a place to sleep and eat. It became an extension of la chica moderna's identity, a space in which women were invited to express their individual style. After the cooking and cleaning and child rearing were taken care of, a woman might sit at her writing desk wearing an exotic dressing gown and catch up on her correspondence with family and friends.

Hollywood and fashion manufacturers teamed up to market Hollywood fashions and establish fashion "tie-ups" with Hollywood films and actresses. Department stores from Los Angeles to New York carried dress styles copied from popular films and a chain of dress boutiques, Cinema Fashion, opened across the United States in the 1930s.[9] Fashion advertisements celebrated dress style as a mode of self-fashioning, characters in films "modeled" modern fashion and modern ways to be, and movie stars promoted fashion in advertisements and through their appearance in articles and news stories about the modern lives of fashionable movie stars. Manufacturers of Ponds cold cream, Ivory Soap, Listerine, and Max Factor makeup recruited American actresses to advertise their products. French designers and ready-to-wear manufacturers employed Norma Shearer, Lupe Velez, and Greta Garbo to model their newest designs. Weekly articles in popular Mexican magazines published in Mexico City also featured young starlets from Warner Bros., Paramount, and 20th Century Fox promoting hairstyles, the latest Paris and New York fashion, makeup, and the modern woman's lifestyle. Hedy Lamarr, one of MGM's most marketable commodities, models "the new

24. The MGM star Hedy Lamarr models the newest lipstick color from Max Factor, *Todo*, 20 November 1934, unpaginated.

25. All Mexican women use Palmolive Soap, including the beautiful Mexican movie star, *Sucesos para Todos*, 20 January 1935, 194.

lipstick, 'True Color' of Hollywood" in *Todo*. Lamarr's face dominates the ad (figure 24, above); it is bigger even than the tube of lipstick, suggesting that the commodity that's being sold is a particular movie-star kind of beauty that can be achieved simply by using the right makeup.

Occasionally, Mexican readers were offered a "national" Hollywood model exemplified by stars that had "made" it in the American movie industry. María Luisa Zea, testifies to her compatriots that "of all the soaps that I have used, only Palmolive keeps my skin smooth" (figure 25, above). In addition to utilizing a Mexican celebrity, the ad addresses Mexican women directly by insisting that "all Mexican women, as well as beautiful new stars" understand that the ingredients of Palmolive soap are totally natural. However, a glance through major Mexican newspapers and popular weekly magazines in the 1920s reveals that although there were regular columns devoted to "Cinematográficas nacionales," "Nuestra cinema," or "El cine mexicano," Hollywood films and Hollywood movie stars dominated film culture in Mexico, exposing Mexican audiences to different worlds and new ways of being.

According to Anne Hollander, "the point about movies is not just that they move, but that they move us." Of course, movies are not the first graphic medium to affect us in this way. Hollander sees motion pictures as "a natural continuation" of earlier artistic practices in the way that they appeal to "unconscious feelings rather than to the conscious intelligence" (1989, 7). She observes, for example, that fashion prints that represented "the new fashions initiated at Versailles were having their effect on everything" (198). Antoine Watteau's seventeenth-century sketches staged people in casual poses that had "the same compelling chic as those created by modern fashion photographers. . . . [It was] both ideally elegant and perfectly natural at the same time. . . . it has looked perfect, but *attainable*." According to Hollander, Watteau's sketches of people "in theatrical costumes, shown mingling with ordinary clothes and unaffected gestures, bring up the modern idea that all clothing is costume, permitting people to fancy themselves playing various parts for each other and for their own private satisfaction" (211). Similarly, the photographs of Ann Southern posing in her backyard in the latest beachwear, lounging in bed with a box of chocolates, and chatting on the phone wearing white pajamas presented an image of attainability to Mexican women who, regardless of their economic status, could imagine themselves as modern. And, the democratic availability of fashion made it possible for many of these women to fantasize themselves as a working woman *and* a mother or a sexually transgressive woman such as May West.

As Hollander explains it, "the cinematic effect of a particular movie star is never merely a function of her body, her skin color, her acting ability, or her dress." Hollander notes that "the Garbo spell, for example, is a matter of light and shade creating an emotional atmosphere analogous to the spell of Vermeer's women, an uncanny evocation of female inwardness" (1989, 445). It wasn't that Mexican women necessarily wanted to look like Garbo, or May West, or Ann Southern, or that these women imagined that by wearing Bette Davis's hairstyle or West's slinky black dress, they would be immediately transformed into a Hollywood movie star. Instead, images of movie stars allowed women the possibility of imagining themselves to be "like" these stars, in terms of being extravagant, fashionable, or sexually transgressive.

It is a given that Hollywood films and Hollywood movie stars dominated Mexican film culture in the 1930s. One might argue that this domination resulted in an "Americanization" of Mexican culture or that the privileging of "modern" U.S. femininity in the promotion of beauty and fashions styles might be seen as an Americanization of femininity. However, such a perspective assumes that femininity is a fixed object that is available for consumption. It also assumes that Mexican women desired to be American and believed that by wearing a particular dress or hairstyle, they could be "American." Jackie Stacey considers that same question in her study of British women's relation to Hollywood movie stars in the 1950s. Her study of female spectators' memories of stars points to "an increasingly interactive relationship between self-image and star ideals with the opening up of multiple possibilities of becoming more like the screen ideal through the purchase of commodities associated with a particular star." She defines this process as "mimetic self-transformation" (236). Rather than seeing this practice as an "intensification of female objectification" or as evidence that British women were simply buying into the "Americanization of British culture," Stacey argues that British women's desire to be and look like Hollywood movie stars indicates "the use of *American* femininity to rebel against what they perceived as restrictive *British* norms" (238).

Similarly, for Mexican women, dress was a tool that was readily available to women across social boundaries that could be used to fashion oneself according to individual interests and desires and in response to different kinds of models. Of course, fashion was not the only thing on women's agendas in Mexico during the 1920s and '30s. Women entered the workforce in markedly increased numbers; they agitated for the right to vote; they worked in the area of social reforms for women and children. Photographs of women involved in social, educational, and cultural spheres were featured daily in the newspapers. The major Mérida paper, *El Diario del Sureste*, had a regular Sunday feature called "Página para las damas" that addressed two full pages to the paper's female readership. The 22 November 1930 issue included two poems written by women, and a number of "serious" articles — including "Breve psicología del amor moderna" and "Musa femenina" — as well as articles devoted to fashion and homemaking.[10]

But, fashion was important to Mexican women. It is a mistake to dismiss fashion and women's concern with fashion as merely a product or effect of capitalism or to reduce women's appropriation of fashion to a consumerist ethic.[11] Fashion codes are not merely imposed upon individuals by the forces of the market. We need to understand women's continued fascination with fashion, the pleasures fashion provides for women, and the ways in which women use fashion to articulate identities. Fashion offers women an opportunity to mark out an identity within certain social and economic constraints: to articulate their social roles, to define their femininity, and to assert an individual identity. They selected different modes of dress for different roles: domestic chores, working outside the home, entertaining. And they made use of fashion to satisfy aesthetic, imaginative, and erotic desires. Perhaps some Mexican women used fashion as a way of rebelling against what they saw as patriarchal structures of femininity. Perhaps others saw dress as a way of promoting their sexuality. Certain women may have chosen dress styles that advertised professional or economic success. And, some women may have *wanted* to project themselves as "Americanized." Fashion styles do not mean the same thing to all women and have no meaning in and of themselves; their significance is produced in relation to the social body they adorn and in relation to social context in which they are appropriated and infused with meaning. In their choice of fashion styles, women take part in the social transformation of gender and gendered identities.

If the public critics cited lamented the new fashion as destructive of an "essential femininity," many women embraced fashion with pleasure. Ultimately, it is impossible to know for sure if a woman bobbed her hair to make a political statement or because short hair was aesthetically pleasing to her or because she wanted to be seen as fashionable in the public eye. The point is that despite the various motives that may have inspired individual decision making in relation to personal appearance, political significance was attached to certain fashion expressions such as bobbed hair, short skirts, and spiked heels. In this sense, we may regard fashion as a discourse and practice through which society as a whole and individuals in particular negotiate their way through a shifting social landscape.

Through their participation in the market economy of everyday life, women responded to and negotiated with dominant discourses of femininity. Rejecting the notion that consumption is merely a response to ideological manipulation, feminist historians have defined the sphere of consumption as a space in which women negotiate the social "truths" of femininity. Rita Felski, for example, criticizes feminist approaches that articulate an "unpredictable yet curiously passive femininity seduced by the glittering phantasmagoria of an emerging consumer culture" (1995, 62). Instead, Felski calls for an understanding of consumption that recognizes individual agency or the ways in which women give meaning to products within the context of their own, everyday lives. In this way, consumption is understood more broadly as an individual response to a hegemony that is constructed through an alliance between the marketplace and other institutions of social control. Dressing up may not have constituted a significant or long-lasting political form of resistance; however, it is obvious from the above discussion that women's decisions about what to wear every morning played a part in the renegotiation of gender in postrevolutionary Mexico.

Chapter 3

Domesticating la Chica Moderna

In Mexico, as in most Western nations, the milieu of Mexican women's
modern everyday life was defined by attendant structures of marriage,
motherhood, and homemaking, structures that were intimately and ir-
revocably connected. This milieu was, of course not so very different
from previous structures of women's daily life. What was different, however, was its location within the ideology of Mexican nationalism and the
framework of consumer capitalism. A concern with the role of women as
mother, nurturer, and protector of moral values was central to the formation of the new nation. At the same time, the story of Mexican modernity
and modernization in relation to women was, to a significant extent, a
story of the relationship between the home and the marketplace. By
1900, the culture of consumption was conjoined with the culture of
domesticity so that in addition to cleaning and cooking, it was the housewife's responsibility to oversee the consumption of material goods that
would benefit home and family.

The first image in this chapter (figure 26) illustrates this understand-

26. The primary job of the modern mother was to oversee her family's consumption habits, *Excelsior*, 19 July 1925, 6.

ing of the relation between family life and the marketplace. The advertisement for Kellogg's Cornflakes envisions a sentimental relation between mother and child. The scene is calm, ordered, and situated in the private space of the home. The mother's "job" is to oversee her child's consuming practices by buying the tastiest and most healthy breakfast cereal. Her ability to manage the family's purchasing habits is the housewife's primary responsibility. This chapter looks at how popular visual culture imagined the modern Mexican wife and housewife and, by extension, the modern Mexican family and home. We will see that *la chica moderna* was defined not merely by her short hair and short skirt but also by the ways in which she occupied and used the gendered space of the home, and through her participation in the marketplace in the service of home and family. I concentrate on a specific category of visual images addressed to women that circulated in the popular culture of a predominantly middle-class consumer: advertisements that promoted the cult of domesticity. I consider how discourses of modernity advised women about contemporary progressive child-rearing theories, and encouraged them to fill their modern homes with the latest in furniture design and cooking and cleaning gadgets. However, despite these very visible aspects of modern life, the modern cult of domesticity was, in many ways, quite similar to the domestic Ideals of the nineteenth century. ⟨similar⟩

These ideals that ordered Mexican family life entailed a separation of work and home, public and private, male and female work and space.[1] The home, commanded by the wife and mother, was defined as personal, intimate, and private; while the public sphere of labor, commerce, and politics was where the husband operated. In order to rationalize this division of labor, women's housework was conceived of as central to family life as the husband's wages. The philosophical underpinnings of modern domesticity were an effect of industrial capitalism and an emerging market economy that distinguished between productive male wage labor and female unpaid (and thus unproductive) household labor. I am not suggesting that the philosophical distinction between public and private spheres should guide our analysis of women's experience of modernity. The notion that the public and the private are distinct and, moreover, are gendered is itself ideological. However, we mustn't lose sight of the fact that women have historically been responsible for housework, whether they took care of their own home, supervised a staff of women servants, or worked as a domestic servant.

While upper-class women made decisions about the household budget and family economy, expenditures, and the management of the house, they had servants to do much of the manual labor. According to Ann Shelby Blum, "the 1910 census counted more than thirty-five thousand women working as domestics" in Mexico City. Although this number dropped significantly after the war (as did wages), middle-class women still hired lower-class women to do "the dirty work" as they turned their attentions to domestic "management (2004, 69–70). Many urban lower-class women and rural women involved in agricultural-related industries worked outside of the home, and few owned labor-saving devices such as washing machines and vacuum cleaners. Notwithstanding the grim realities of the lives of most women, however, all women were urged by the market and the state to conform to the ideal of middle-class domesticity. If class determined the extent to which women could voluntarily participate in the practice of modern domesticity, and if domesticity was essentially an ideology of middle-classness, its ideals filtered down into the homes of working-class and rural women and became a model of modern life to aspire to.

William French writes that "by the time of the Porfiriato, so powerful was the ideal of the domestic role of women" that, for some, a family's social rank was ascribed to the "'moral' behavior of women" (1996, 87–89). Similar to the nineteenth-century British and North American ideal of "True Womanhood," the virtues of piety, purity, submissiveness, and domesticity characterized the Mexican housewife. In 1869, Catherine Beecher (sister of the American suffragette, Harriet Beecher Stowe), codified a modern cult of domesticity with the publication of *The American Woman's Home: On Principles of Domestic Science*. Beecher's advice book advocated homemaking as women's rightful labor, decreed "by Nature and God," influencing a new generation of homemakers around the world. This social view of womanhood was informed by existing scientific understandings of gender. In the nineteenth century, the medical establishment insisted that women were biologically adapted to "the sacred role of homemaker" (Shuttleworth, 55). In the 1920s and '30s, women in Mexico were governed by similar discourses of domesticity that defined the home as a "natural" space of femininity.

Although I focus on the role of the market in the chapter, I recognize that the modernizing of domesticity was not solely a marketing ploy: the state conceived of it as central to the modernization of the nation. In other words, what was good for the family was good for the nation, and visa versa. Article 123 of the 1917 Mexican Constitution granted women pregnancy and childbirth benefits, but it did not address significant labor issues of concern to women such as equal opportunity, maternal leave, or child care. And while the state mandated increased educational opportunities for women, much of this education was concerned with the disciplines of home economics and family health care. For example, in the 1920s, educators were sent out into urban working-class neighborhoods and rural villages to instruct women in modern methods of keeping house and raising children for the benefit of the nation. In addition to reading, writing, and arithmetic, a major emphasis of this educational campaign was on *los anexos*, or additional activities that included training in domestic skills and knowledge such as hygiene, nutrition, gardening, and weaving (Meyers, 37–38).

The primary player in the domestication of la chica moderna, however, was the marketplace. In July 1924, the weekly illustrated magazine *Revista de Revistas* introduced a new section, "El hogar moderno." The editor suggests that after a century of struggle, Mexicans were now ready to return to the tranquility of the home that, "in the spirit of our tradition and our heritage, we insist on" (13 July, 7). Subsequent issues featured articles about *la cocina moderna*, *la alcoba moderna*, and *la sala moderna*. Photographs of modern kitchens, bedrooms, and living rooms illustrated these articles, while advertisements throughout the magazine promoted cleaning agents, furniture, and household technologies. In the editorial, *Revista de Revistas* imagined a new community of Mexicans who share a middle-class history and middle-class ideals about the centrality of *la casa* in modern life. This kind of popular philosophizing is an example of nation building that occurs alongside that of official, state-sponsored legislating. While journalists, businessmen, and advertising executives did not explicitly collude with the state to coordinate their commercial campaigns with political and social nationalizing projects, in general, the commercial discourse aligned with the state discourse around family, domesticity, and the role of women.

As discussed earlier, gendered spatial patterns are produced through the activation of economic, ideological, and social discourses. Domestic spaces came to be understood as private, family spaces as opposed to public spaces occupied by crowds of unrelated people. The home was a feminized space of consumption of food and other commodity products. Within the space of the home, practices informed by social discourses of gender take place. The family kitchen, now imagined as a distinct space and modernized through the introduction of technological inventions such as electricity and running water, became the center of women's lives, despite the fact that most Mexican homes — especially rural homes — did not have separate rooms for cooking. But, the modern kitchen was not solely a room for cooking; it was a feminized location in which women were pictured acting out the socially proscribed role of housewife. It was a productive space — women were generally pictured as cooking or cleaning, performing "women's work."

In the women's section of *El Heraldo Ilustrado* a well-dressed mother teaches her daughter the art of cooking in the gendered space of her *cocina moderna* (figure 27). The stove is the centerpiece of the composition. It defines both the work of women and the space in which that work is undertaken. In addition to learning how to cook an elegant meal on a modern stove, the little girl, who wears an apron that matches her mother's, is mastering the basics of becoming a modern housewife. Reading this illustration as a narrative, we understand that she will grow up to be like and engage in the same gendered practices as her mother. As this image illustrates, representations of domestic life "sold" ideals of modern lifestyles as much as they sold commercial products.

Selling Domesticity

The primary function of modern advertising was to promote a culture of consumption that identified a way of being in the modern world. Advertisements sold household commodities of course, but at the same

LA COCINA MODERNA

MENU DE HOY

SOPA DE YEMAS.—Se deshacen quince yemas de huevo en cuatro cuartillos de caldo colado; éste se pone a cocer en baño María: cuando haya cuajado se va poniendo en cucharaditas en una sopera. Ya para servirse se le pone el caldo y una poca de pimienta en polvo.

con un pedazo de pan se rocían y bajan del metate con vinagre y poca agua, se frien en manteca y sazonan con azúcar y canela molida; fuera de la lumbre se les pone poco aceite y granos de granada.

CONSOMÉ.—En cuatro cuartillos de agua se ponen: una libra de pulpa, una libra de jarrete, una pata de ternera, una gallina, seis zanahorias, unos garbanzos, un poquito de arroz, dos cebollas y una ramita de perejil.

Se deja hervir hasta que se reduzca el caldo a un cuartillo, se desgrasa y ya para servirlo se le pone una cucharada de vino Jerez.

AGUACATES RELLENOS.—Se escogen que no sean de los redondos que tienen el hueso grande ni de los muy largos que no pueden quedar parados; partidos por la mitad, (pero no a lo largo), para sacarles el hueso, se pelan y rellenan de picadillo; se ponen en el platón por lo más plano y se cubren con lo siguiente; peladas las nueces y molidas juntamente

LOMO FRIO MOLIDO.—Se muele una libra de lomo de puerco, un pedazo de longaniza, un puño de pasas, otro de almendras, bastante clavo y pimienta. A esto se le mezclan tres yemas de huevo, un cuarto de vino Jerez, una poca de mantequilla y se pone al horno.

LECHE DE ALMENDRAS.—Seis cuartillos de leche se endulzan al gusto y se les ponen seis yemas de huevo deshechas en leche y cuatro onzas de almendras muy molidas; se pone esto a la lumbre; cuando tome punto se le agregan otras cuatro onzas de almendra tostada y martajada como arroz, se deja que dé unos tres hervores; se vacía en un platón, poniéndole encima polvo de azúcar, al día siguiente se le dora.

27. Teaching one's daughter how to be "una mujer decente,"
El Heraldo Ilustrado, 23 May 1920, unpaginated.

¡A 10 Centavos el Pan!

Ahora usted puede lavar sus vestidos y
artículos de franela, de hilo, de seda y de
lana con el legítimo jabón de lavar Crystal
White, comúnmente conocido por jabón
CHIVO o BORREGO.

Lava sus Vajillas de Loza y Cristalería con el Jabón Crystal White.

28. Advertising and the gendered space of the modern home, *Excelsior*, 31 May 1928, 5.

time, they shaped social understandings of housework and of housewives through the visual production of a gendered social life. Advertising worked to map out a place for women in the gendered space of the
modern home and in the role of the modern housewife (figure 28,
above). If men were the primary wage earner in the modern, middle-
class household, women were wage spenders, charged with feeding,
clothing, and cleaning their households. Within this world, the private
space of the home increasingly assumed a more important social role as
wives and mothers were urged to purchase items necessary to make their
homes attractive centers of family lives. Domestic tasks were performed
by women, homemaking products were exclusively pitched to women,
and shopping was configured as a way of legitimizing a woman's essential social role. The lady of the house was encouraged to purchase the
newest Electrolux or Eureka vacuum cleaner because it was her duty as a
wife and mother to maintain the cleanliness of the house according to
the most up-to-date methods.

While advertisers worked with producers to develop systematic advertising campaigns aimed at differentiating one brand from another, the

campaigns were also designed to create consumer demand and thus markets for manufactured goods by demonstrating how a glass cleaner or a new Electrolux vacuum would transform the housewife's life and make her happier. Ads promised women that a product was easy to use and labor saving, and pictured the work of the housewife as easy, undemanding, and enjoyable. The ads in figures 29 and 30 ignore the labor involved in housecleaning while accentuating qualities such as cleanliness and order, ease of use, and pleasurable rewards. Neither woman is engaged in backbreaking manual labor. According to the ads, housework was not really "work" at all. The advertisement for Electrolux features a well-dressed modern woman sweeping her lightweight, easy-to-use vacuum cleaner effortlessly across a small rug. An ad for the household cleaner, Bon Ami, reflects the ecstatic face of another housewife engaged in the joyful experience of cleaning her mirror. The accompanying text suggests that the job takes little effort, informing the reader that she only needs to apply a "light coating of Bon Ami, let it dry for a moment, and remove," and her glass mirror will be "splendid."

As discussed in chapter 1, the commerce of household commodities circulating throughout Mexico immediately after the revolution was dominated by European and U.S. manufacturers and advertising industries.[2] While some Mexican industries — such as tobacco, beer, steel, and explosives — retained monopolistic control over the domestic market, the majority of consumer products advertised in the Mexican media — such as Electrolux vacuums and Bon Ami cleansers — were "made in America," at least until 1929.[3] The foreign control of the marketplace was ideological as much as it was economic. To a large extent, Euro-American visions of a bourgeois, middle-class lifestyle shaped homemaking practices and the design and furnishing of the home, and it was this transnational modern life that was being sold to Mexican housewives along with bathroom cleansers and electric mixers. Well-designed and well-decorated rooms were assigned dedicated uses: a living room for entertaining, a kitchen for cooking, and a dining room for sharing meals with the family.

The Mexican press featured ads for foreign household products that ranged from toothpaste to cleaning solutions. These products, once produced in the home or on the farm, were now mass-produced and widely available in packaged form in the corner store and through mail-order

29. Modern housecleaning is "effortless" and enjoyable, *Sucesos para Todos*, 14 July 1933, unpaginated.

30. The joyful experience of housecleaning, *Revista de Revistas*, 3 January 1926, 9.

catalogues. United States manufacturers of consumer goods expanded their reach to lucrative foreign markets to increase their customer base and their profits, and by the early 1920s American-made products dominated the advertising pages of Mexican mass media. In *Advertising for Trade in Latin-America*, published in 1922, W. E. Aughinbaugh, an American expert in international trade, advised U.S. business that "there are approximately sixty-six million people in Latin-America, a number so great and with potential resources and purchasing power so colossal that the commercial eyes of the entire world are centered on" those countries (4). Aughinbaugh understood that the "assumption that what appeals to an American will appeal to a Brazilian, an Argentinean or a Chilean" was false and would lead to the failure of American advertisers to reach those consumers (10). He encouraged advertisers to research their markets, pointing out that they wasted a lot of money promoting home electric appliances without realizing that few houses in Latin America were wired for electricity. While North American companies such as Frigidaire, General Electric, and Westinghouse did recognize they were addressing a different market, they also understood that they were not just selling household products.

Like fashion advertisements, the promotion of household technologies and commodities emphasized novelty and individual expressiveness and appealed to individual desire and fantasy, but also drew from scientific and business discourses of rationality and efficiency. Another book by Beecher, *A Treatise on Domestic Economy*, published in 1843, proposed the idea of a modern "model kitchen" based on ideas of hygiene, ergonomics, and efficiency. At the turn of the century, modern theories of homemaking, specified by particular standards of cleanliness and scientific management, were introduced to middle-class housewives all over the world.[4] In the United States, the American Home Economics Association (AHEA) was formally organized in 1909 with the aim of improving "living conditions in the home, the institutional household, and the community," according to page 1 of the first volume of the *Journal of Home Economics*, published that same year.[5]

Scientific discourse made the home into a workplace, highlighting professionalism, efficiency, organization, hygiene, technology, and progress. Mary Pattison published *The Principles of Domestic Management* in 1915.

Christine Frederick's *The New Housekeeping: Efficiency Studies in Home Management* (1916) became the housekeeping "bible" for millions of women all over the world. *The New Housekeeping* expanded Beecher's thesis by outlining a sustained explanation of the "science of domesticity." Frederick learned about theories of business management efficiency through discussions with her husband and his business associates and decided to bring this science into the home. Frederick, in fact, first introduced the concept of the housewife as "purchasing agent" (102). Following on Frederick's heels, advice columnists and ad copy writers served as "translators" or "mediators between companies and consumers." These translators reinforced the idea that women were keepers of the hearth, encouraged women to shop wisely, explained why hygiene was important, and instructed housewives on how to use specific products and appliances, resorting to terms such as *science, cleanliness,* and *thriftiness* to validate their expertise. Advertisements emphasized that an efficient and economical household could be achieved through a well-organized work environment and the use of tools and mechanized appliances designed especially for the modern home.

One of the most important concepts of the new science of domesticity was that of "home hygiene," which was conceived of as a way to ensure the physical and moral health of home, self, and family. Initially a set of theories developed by the international medical profession for the establishment of public health policies following the pioneering work of Louis Pasteur, hygienic principles were quickly appropriated to ensure codes of "respectability" in the private sphere (Stewart, 56–59).[6] The "importance of cleaning as a household task" did not just appear in the twentieth century. Caroline Davidson notes that "between about 1670 and 1820 the status of cleaning was transformed; it ceased to be a peripheral aspect of housework and became one of central importance (128). What differentiated modern domestic hygiene from earlier understandings of the "clean home" was its intimate connection to a woman's success as a modern homemaker. In addition to the promotion of beauty products that would ensure individual health, household cleaning soaps and over-the-counter tonics for treating family health issues were promoted to the housewife so that she could protect her family's well-being. Public campaigns and ads for specific cleaning products

La mujer moderna . . . . .
necesita **MODES**

representa un gran adelanto en toallas sanitarias

SIEMPRE de compras . . . de visita . . . de paseo, y debiendo siempre sentirse cómoda y segura de conservar su pulcritud en toda época. Por eso es que la mujer moderna ha abandonado los antiguos e inseguros métodos higiénicos y ha adoptado Modess, la nueva toalla sanitaria de incomparable comodidad.

La almohadilla de Modess está hecha de copos suaves y absorbentes de una substancia parecida al algodón pero que se disuelve en agua corriente. La gasa que la envuelve está ligeramente acolchada para hacerla más suave y cómoda. Uno de los lados es impermeable, para que su protección sea más eficaz. Y está hecha de acuerdo con la moda de trajes ajustados y telas vaporosas para que no se note en uso.

Su garantía de calidad la da la firma de Johnson & Johnson afamada hace cerca de medio siglo en la fabricación de artículos sanitarios e higiénicos.

Todas las buenas farmacias y tiendas de ropa venden Modess.

· **MODESS** ·
LA TOALLA SANITARIA MODERNA

31. Female cleanliness made public, *Ilustrado*, 31 October 1929, 43.

warned women of the dangers associated with dirt and filth. With this emphasis on cleanliness, issues never before discussed were now made available for public discussion. Body odor, athlete's foot, digestive problems, bathroom habits, and menstruation were on display in advertisements and advice columns (figure 31, above).

The emergence of the "cult of cleanliness" was not merely a function of scientific rationale but was "founded on new technologies and structured by new economic forms and new consumer rituals" (Sivulka 2001, 13). In other words, the marketplace adopted the language of science to encourage the consumption of household cleaning products. Cleanliness was linked to morality, to status, to gender roles, and the economic well-being of family and nation. Patience Schell traces the development of an official cult of cleanliness in Mexico from the Porfirian era through postrevolutionary practice. She finds that a decidedly continuous thesis of middle-class respectability dominated the Mexican hygiene movement from the end of the nineteenth century through the 1930s. During that period, the state and the medical establishment promoted the ideal of "a self-sacrificing mother caring for dutiful children in a tidy, sanitary home," and mothers who failed in their duty were subject to state intervention (2004, 573).

According to the state and to the marketplace, a mother's duty to the nation and her family was to ensure a clean and safe home. The state implemented a number of nationwide health programs aimed at mothers that promoted the relation between clean homes and moral homes. Women were instructed in modern methods of infant care and housekeeping techniques. For example, a document published in 1921 by the School of Hygiene Service entitled "The Child" offered Mexican mothers "instructions on how to properly clean hands, rooms, and clothing, excise microbes, breastfeed, and disinfect the kitchen and bathroom" (A. M. Stern, 376). Although most women lived in homes without heat, running water, or indoor plumbing, and baths and clean clothes were hard to come by, a sanitized house and family were regarded as fundamental to the health of family and nation. Soap was central to this ideology of cleanliness.

The modern soap industry was intimately connected to the domestic hygiene movement. In the United States, the Association of American Soap and Glycerin Producers established the Cleanliness Institute in the 1920s "to teach the public the importance of keeping clean." Modern home technologies made the home "cleaner than ever before." Soap industry campaigns advertised soaps for cleaning bodies and floors through pictures of homemakers washing floors, windows, and babies. Women were further reminded that a woman's beauty was first and foremost clean (Vinkas, 79–83).[7] In this way, cleanliness was connected to a woman's spiritual purity, her virtue, and her femininity.

Advertising strategies for selling home and personal cleaning agents visibly emphasized cleanliness, economy, and the quality of "being modern" and included words such as "clean, scientific, economical, and safe." An ad for Flytox (figure 32) warns housewives that cockroaches, mosquitos, and flies can deposit "noxious germs" in food. The ad's text informed readers that Flytox's formula was "very scientific . . . [and]

32. Clean, scientific,
economical, and safe,
Revista de Revistas,
3 January 1926, 10.

manufactured after many studies and experiments by the Mellon Institute." Yet, advertisers did not want to alarm women by insinuating that only a scientist could safely handle Flytox. Indeed, the ad assures consumers that the product is "very easy and very safe" by picturing an ordinary young housewife in the role of a bug killer.

Other product promotions stressed that health and cleanliness were a mother's primary responsibility: an ad for Lydia Pinkham's Compuesto Vegetal (Vegetable Compound) reminds young mothers of their duty to maintain "balanced health" for the well-being of their firstborn child (figure 33). The illustration attracts its female addressee with an image of a mother and child but also resorts to another popular marketing strategy: the use of testimonials by women who experienced unqualified success with the product. While Lydia Pinkham was a North American

33. The use of testimonials by "ordinary" housewives and mothers was a popular and effective advertising strategy, *Revista de Revistas*, 7 October 1923, 58.

company that marketed its products all over the world, in this ad it directly addresses its Mexican audience by speaking to her in Spanish and by including the testimonial of a Mexican woman. In the bottom right-hand corner, María Hernández from Vera Cruz, Mexico, relates her heartbreaking history and gives permission to publish her story: "Three of my children were stillborn and the other a miscarriage. After I took the Compound, I gave birth to a precious and healthy baby."

Housecleaning was further modernized through the promotion of the "wonders" of technology. Advertisers worked to convince housewives that they "needed" washing machines and vacuum cleaners, that these appliances were necessities and not just luxuries. Women were encouraged to educate themselves on the use of electrical appliances that facilitated modern methods of accomplishing household tasks. One of the earliest ads for an electric appliance for home use I found was in a 1916 edition of the women's magazine *El Hogar*. The issue featured an advertisement for "Electromotor, S. A.," promoting the "best American brand of electric flat irons." By the 1920s, Mexican women who could afford them could purchase household appliances such as *planchas eléctricas* (electric irons), *hornos eléctricos* (electric ovens), and *frigidaires* that were guaranteed to be safe, economical, and timesaving. These appliances even found their way into small towns and villages. In Robert Redfield's description of the material culture of the village of Tepoztlán in the late 1920s, for example, he notes that while by no means pervasive, "a conspicuous minority" of households "enjoy elements of modern industrial civilization" (39). And by the 1930s, in areas far from Mexico City, such as the Yaqui Valley region in the northern state of Sonora, housewives had access to all the accessories of urban modernity, including "pain relievers, sewing machines, and Sears catalogues" (Vaughan 2000, 204).

According to advertisements and advice columns, the ideal home was an electric home. Electricity was introduced into the urban home in Europe and the United States in the early 1900s, but even then it was not widespread.[8] Electric washing machines and electric vacuum cleaners were introduced in 1908. Households were slow to adapt technology powered by electricity, in part because of cost, but also because many families weren't convinced that this technology was necessary. In Mexico City at the turn of the century, electric tramways traversed the streets and electric lamps lit up the main avenues. Upper-class *colonias* were "equipped with all the amenities of modern life including electricity, drainage, running water, and telephones" (Piccato, 20–21). However, in reality, only a small percentage of households could afford electrical appliances. In order to increase demand, the industry realized it would have to teach consumers that domestic electrical appliances were vital for the modern home. Carolyn Marvin describes how advertising campaigns focused on electricity's "beauty, purity, brightness, cleanliness, and safety" (76). Education in the form of advertising addressed to middle- and upper-class women claimed that electric-powered technology would "help a woman become a better housewife," would reduce the amount of physical labor involved in housework and thus free up women to spend more time with their families, and would reduce dependency and thus save money on domestic hired help. The ad campaigns also appealed to the discourse of sanitation by claiming that "electrical appliances would make the home 'germ-free'" (Bowden and Offer, 265–66).

One of the challenges for advertisers was to convince women that domesticity could be a pleasurable pastime and would "greatly reduce the labor involved in cooking, cleaning, sewing, washing, scrubbing, or whatever" (Norris, 80). Appropriating modern aesthetics from the art world, they pictured cleaning, cooking, and child care as enjoyable activities that would be enhanced by modern products and appliances. An ad for a store called Sala de Electricidad in the October/December 1928 issues of *Mexican Folkways* insisted that "electricity is the most valuable aid for the women of the house" because it allows her to complete all her tasks and still have time for leisure activities. The signed lithograph features a modern woman dressed in a knee-length daytime dress, high heels, a fur stole, and a cloche hat over her bobbed hair; in the background is a smaller tableau of family life that shows the housewife cooking on an electric stove, vacuuming, ironing, reading by electric light, and serving coffee to her husband from an electric coffee pot (192).

An interesting example of promotion of technology to the modern housewife is the sewing machine. The introduction of the mechanical sewing machine in the nineteenth century is generally linked to the rapid expansion of the garment industry (Coffin, 759). As Judith G. Coffin points out, however, sewing machine manufacturers were also intent on marketing the machine as a "domestic" appliance. And, even though initially sewing machines had "many possible destinations or markets," Coffin argues, advertising immediately developed campaigns that spoke to gendered audiences: "Specialized machines" were advertised to men and to industry, while "'family' models" were aimed at women (758–59).

While women had been working as *costureras*, or seamstresses, in Mexico's clothing industry since the late 1900s, sewing machines had not yet been introduced as a household technology. In addition to working in factories and subcontracting workshops, women also worked as subcontractors or as pieceworkers out of their home. Although the work was often highly skilled, it was done by hand and thus labor intensive

34. A tableau
of modern
motherhood,
*Revista de
Revistas*
(Mexico City),
2 September
1923, 23.

and wages were low. Because sewing was associated with lower-class
working women and with wage labor, the sewing machine had to be
"retooled" in order to appeal to middle-class women. Manually operated
sewing machines, although expensive, were first offered for home use in
Europe and the United States in the late 1800s. By the turn of the
century, electrically powered, more affordable sewing machines were
widely available. According to Sarah Gordon's study of the promotion
and diffusion of the home sewing machine in early-twentieth-century
United States, sewing was imbued with "understandings of femininity,
family, and social class. It evoked ideas about thrift, housekeeping, wifely
duty, motherly love, and sexual attraction" (68). Women were encouraged to sew for their families in order to save money while at the same
time articulating their own creativity and individual style.

Ads for sewing machines in Mexico proposed the same ideas as demonstrated by the advertisement for a "New Home Sewing Machine"
depicted in figure 34 (above). The scene situates a young mother safely
in the context of her home so that readers would not mistake her activity
as "work." The focus of the ad is not on the machine itself but on the
woman's relationship to her child. The sewing machine, in fact, occupies
a secondary importance in the narrative of the image. According to this

ad, the only purpose of the machine is to make the housewife a "better" mother. At the same time, however, enterprising women realized the economic possibilities of investing in one of these new home industrial machines. According to interviews Josiah McC. Heyman collected from women who grew up in Sonora in the 1920s, while American-made sewing machines were expensive, they were "a universal item in every mine worker and middle class family." Furthermore, the women who managed the sewing machine "drew on the Sears catalog" to produce articles of clothing for themselves and their families "based on Euro-American fashions" (160–61).

Designing Domesticity

Modern domesticity was not simply concerned with the tasks of maintaining home and family. Commodity culture made the home into an extension of a woman's essential self, not merely a thing that she took care of. Home decorating was a way housewives could work actively to produce a modern middle-class identity for herself and her family. An ad for the newest model of the Coleman gas stove (figure 35), for example, offers female consumers a way to envision themselves as modern as they engage in the tasks of everyday homemaking. Unlike traditional Mexican kitchens, with their wood-fired ovens and clay pots (figure 36), or the dirt floors and stone mortar and pestles found in the homes of poor rural families, the modern, economical kitchen boasted a small, gas stove; an electric refrigerator; gleaming stainless steel cooking utensils; an easy-to-clean linoleum floor; and an electric "sweeper" or vacuum cleaner to supplant the handmade straw broom. Most important, there is nothing particularly "Mexican" about la cocina moderna; it could be located almost anywhere in the modern, developed world.

The Coleman stove advertisement addresses women directly through a number of aesthetic and discursive strategies: It suggests that this is "the stove *you've* always wished for." It presents a figure of identification for viewers to relate to in terms of gender (if not class or race), and that figure of identification turns her gaze onto the viewer as if engaged in a private conversation. While the text that accompanies the image

La Estufa Que Usted Tanto Ha Deseado

35. Modern
housewives use
modern stoves,
Universal,
6 May 1928, 2.

36. A woman making tortillas without the benefit of a modern gas oven,
reproduced as a postcard. Courtesy of Susan Toomey Frost, uncredited
hand-tinted photograph.

promotes the stove as "clean, sanitary, economical, and easy to use," it also appeals to the modern young housewife's sense of style and taste. Like the woman in the Electrolux ad, this woman is dressed for an afternoon of shopping or visiting with her friends. And her kitchen, with its brand-new stove and gleaming linoleum floor, reflects her fashionable and modern taste. Even if a female reader didn't have the desire for or need of a new kitchen appliance, she could always fantasize about being the happy, well-dressed woman in the ad.

Shopping was constituted as a legitimate form of self-expression for the dutiful wife and mother. According to Tiersten, "agents of the market — advertisers, department store managers, fashion journalists, self-styles taste experts — played a particularly decisive role in reinventing consumption as an art form and making the resource of taste broadly available to the bourgeois consumer public" (7–8). Advertisements and advice columns that proliferated in popular magazines and in the women's pages of daily newspapers emphasized the gratifications available for women through the designing and decorating of the modern home. In addition to being thrifty, housewives needed to develop a modern sense of taste in order to become an "artist-consumer" (Tiersten, 186). Economic and social change was accompanied by transformations in the aesthetic realm. Bourgeoisie taste emerged as a sign of cultural refinement. In other words, it was not so much the commodities themselves that defined one as middle class, but rather the "taste" or aesthetic sensibility of the consumer that was reflected in her choice of products and in the interior design of her home.

The middle-class consumer's sense of "taste" was the target of advertisers, interior decorators, and industrial designers. In her study of refrigerator design, Shelley Nickles finds that industrial designers interpreted this consumer as a "servantless housewife" and that she was "the source of design standards for the entire product line of refrigerators." The middle-class housewife's taste privileged attributes of "modernity, beauty, economy, hygiene, and household provisioning" (699). Refrigerators designers selected white as the signifier of cleanliness and sanitation and promoted this ideal through illustrations and ad copy. Households were made to see that "by buying a white refrigerator and keeping it in the kitchen, the housewife expressed her awareness of modern sanitary and food preservation standards; her ability to keep the refrigerator white and devoid of dirt represented the extent to which she met these standards" (705).

The dutiful mother need not worry that her consuming practices were merely a form of narcissistic entertainment. Design was central to the formation of the modern home. Catherine Beecher insisted that a well-designed home should be "healthful, economical, and tasteful." Moreover, "time, labor, and expense are saved" through the design of the house itself, as well as through the arrangement of the furniture (1869, 133–35). As discussed earlier, Frederick's *The New Housekeeping* also emphasized efficiency and order but incorporated the language of modernity. Frederick's ideas were to have a profound effect on the design layout of the modern kitchen through simple observations such as "Did we not waste time and needless walking in poorly arranged kitchens?" (quoted in Freeman, 29–30). However, as June Freeman notes, it was the European modernist movement that gave this ideal of efficiency its modern aesthetic, writing that "European functionalism provided a concrete design style which visually complemented the 'scientific' approach to kitchen layout" (33). There were a number of influences that advanced the consumer's interest in the design of everyday material culture, including international design exhibitions, such as the 1925 Paris Exposition Internationale des Arts Décoratifs et Industriels Modernes, advances in advertising technology and display, the explosion of department stores and other retail outlets, and the concurrent modernization of sales techniques (Harris, 66–68).

In Mexico, technological modernity had become a "common sight" by the 1920s and was championed by the Mexican avant-garde, known as *estridentismo* and by artists such as Diego Rivera, who "celebrated the machines of modern industry" in his murals (Gallo, 5–6). Ordinary people also embraced this modernity as more and more middle-class homes acquired telephones, typewriters, and photographic cameras (22–23). Magazines and other publications, *Nuestra Mexico*, for instance, popularized the machine aesthetic through drawings and photographs showcasing the design movement in art and interior design. In the world of design, modernity was opposed to "old-fashionedness." The cluttered, draped, and dark Victorian interiors of nineteenth-century *old*

Mexican bourgeoisie homes had to be restyled to fit into the modern era. Modern design was clean, simple, and uncluttered. In place of open shelving, ceramic tile counters, piles of ceramic cooking pots, and a large wooden eating table, the new kitchen was streamlined. Everything was hidden away behind closed cabinets; all the countertops were built at a uniform height that allowed the average woman to work without bending over; and the kitchen was outfitted with all of the latest mechanical gadgets. Living rooms and bedrooms were similarly planned with a focus on efficiency, simplicity, and design.

The domestic space of the home was characterized as an extension of the housewife's individuality. The illustrated article on *la alcoba moderna* (figure 37), the modern bedroom, visibly ties the modernist styling of the bedroom to modern identities, personified by the flapper and her dapper partner. Each is situated in relation to a vase decorated with modernist, Art Deco motifs. Through activities such as choosing which products to buy and designing the space of the home, the housewife partook in a process of self-fashioning by extending her "uniqueness" beyond the confines of her own body, an artistic practice that women were encouraged to engage with in their primary role as housewives. Design figured in this promotion campaign as producers vied for markets and style functioned to differentiate one manufacturer's product from another. Design was not merely aesthetic packaging, but worked to construct demand, establish hierarchies of taste, and even define a product's purpose and utility. Stylistic choice on the part of the consumer was identified as an articulation of social status, even if the consumer did not occupy that position.

According to Penny Sparke, a theory of design that emerged in the mid-nineteenth century, called the "functionalist tradition," claimed that "manufacturing methods determine not only the means of production but also the forms of the products" (5). This theory was not concerned with "market preferences" but with streamlining and maximizing the production process in line with modern theories of efficiency (5–7). It wasn't until the first decade of the twentieth century that we see "the growth of the relationship of design to marketing." Sparke aligns this growth to major social changes, such as the growth of a middle-class with increased access to discretionary incomes, the expansion of retail

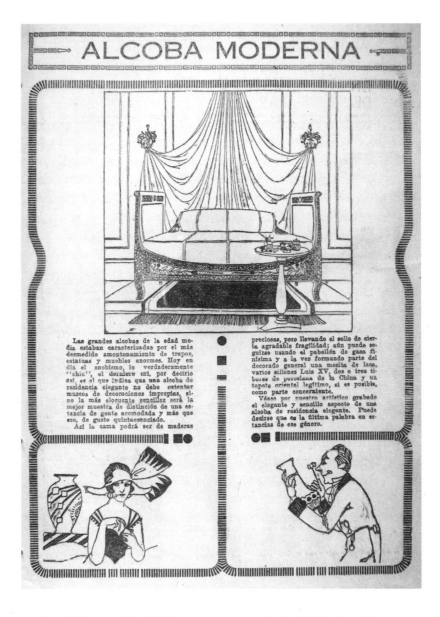

ALCOBA MODERNA

Las grandes alcobas de la edad media estaban caracterizadas por el más desmedido amontonamiento de trapos, estatuas y muebles enormes. Hoy en día el snobismo, lo verdaderamente "chic", el derniere cri, por decirlo así, es el que indica que una alcoba de residencia elegante no debe ostentar museos de decoraciones impropias, sino la más elocuente sencillez será la mejor muestra de distinción de una estancia de gente acomodada y más que eso, de gusto quintaesenciado.

Así la cama podrá ser de maderas preciosas, pero llevando el sello de cierta agradable fragilidad; aún puede seguirse usando el pabellón de gasa finísima y a la vez formando parte del decorado general una mesita de laca, varios sillones Luis XV, dos o tres tibores de porcelana de la China y un tapete oriental legítimo, si es posible, como parte concerniente.

Véase por nuestro artístico grabado el elegante y sencillo aspecto de una alcoba de residencia elegante. Puede decirse que es la última palabra en estancias de ese género.

37. An article on modern bedrooms, presents an "artistic" drawing of an "elegant yet simple bedroom," *El Heraldo Ilustrado*, 6 June 1920, unpaginated.

shops and department stores, and the rise of a professional advertising industry, discussed in the preceding chapter (14). The design strategy for Frigidaires in the late 1920s, for example, switched from focusing on "the refrigerator's primary function, preserving food" to a marketing campaign that linked the refrigerator "visually to the responsibilities of the average housewife to provide a clean, safe environment for her family" by, for example, making all models a "sparkling" and hygienic white (S. Stevens, 705).

Because the home was an idealized extension of a woman's essential self, it became a place for women to be creative, to relax, and to partake in leisure activities. The discourse of fashion that stressed style and aesthetics was incorporated into home decoration. One popular modern design style for the home borrowed from the aesthetics of Art Deco, an international art and design movement popular from 1910 to 1935.[9] While there is no exact definition of Art Deco, because of its eclectic manifestations in fashion and in interior decoration and because it interacted with other design styles, this modernist style is inexorably tied to the idea of commerce and industry, the modern city and urbanity, and influenced by European avant-garde art movements of the teens and twenties such as Constructivism, Futurism, Cubism, and German Expressionism. Art Deco was also shaped by the popularity of "primitive" artistic styles from Egypt, the Middle East, Mexico, and Africa, popular among artists, intellectuals, and art collectors (Fischer, 16–17). In general, it is identified by slender, geometric forms and sharp, zigzag lines, and the incorporation of chrome, glass, and wood.

Although it emerged in fine arts and architecture, internationally — Gallo points to Mexico City's "Art Deco district," Colonia Condesa, built in the 1920s — Art Deco was affixed to modern consumerism through the design and marketing of fashion, interior design, housewares, and the flood of technological household appliances such as sewing machines and refrigerators. Art Deco reinforced the idea that this technology was "modern" in part because it was "universal," one of the first transnational mass-produced styles. Modern theories of home decorating, modern materials, and modern design came together to influence the repackaging of the modern home and, by extension, the modern woman. Terms such as *streamlining*, *youthful*, *contemporary*, *simple*, *comfortable*, and *dust-free* dominated the discourse of advertising (Leavitt, 100–5).

In the context of the production of cultural nationalism in the 1920s, a local aesthetic that combined national and international design elements influenced architecture and interior decoration, as well as the advertising of Mexican-made commodities. Intellectual visionaries and architects such as Juan O'Gorman embraced European design strategies including Art Deco as part of their attempt to create a revolutionary "style" that spoke to the ideologies of the historical moment. This hybrid style also made its appeal in the realm of commodity culture. Advertisements for such mundane products as toothpaste, kitchen cleansers, and home health remedies pictured "real women," either photographed or hand drawn, defined as "Mexican" by their costume or name. An advertisement for a popular Mexican beer, Victoria, (figure 38) relies on the marriage of national icons — the rebozo and the embroidered folkloric skirt — with international design strategies visible in the composition of the image and the choice of font style. A Mexican sewing machine company promotes its National brand with the figure of a woman dressed as *la china poblana* (a "type" detailed in chapter 5) wearing a traditional Mexican costume (figure 39). If the ad for New Home Sewing Machine discussed above conceives of the housewife as a universal figure, producers of the National Sewing Machine saw their consumer as specifically Mexican.

While discussions of *mexicanidad* or a projection of a Mexican authenticity have generally been concerned with political nationalism or with the work of the muralists and its manifestation in the popular arts, the images in this chapter reveal a concrete and contemporary example of the new Mexican woman. She embraced modern theories of domesticity and used household and beauty products that were manufactured according to up-to-date hygienic principles. These images reveal that the logic of the marketplace allowed her to be both modern and Mexican. The choices Mexican women made about what to purchase for themselves and their families articulated their relationship to modernity and modern consumer products and reveal how these women imagined themselves to be la chica moderna within the constraints proscribed.

38. An advertisement for a Mexican beer, Victoria, offers an example of the marriage of national and international design strategies, *Jueves de Excelsior*, 2 August 1923, inside back cover.

39. *La china poblana* promotes a National brand sewing machine," *Jueves de Excelsior*, 10 May 1923, unpaginated.

Through the use of modernistic style, color, and photography, and by positioning "modern" products within the context of a social tableau that promoted modernity, ad creators presented "an ideal modern life" that consumers were encouraged to aspire to (Marchand 1985, xviii). Thus, although advertisements that circulated in Mexico do not tell us how the majority of Mexicans lived their lives, they do offer information as to what kinds of products and lifestyles were promoted to female consumers and therefore illustrate how the global discourse of domesticity contributed to the production of the Mexican chica moderna as a modern, stylish, thrifty, and virtuous consumer.

Chapter 4

Picturing Working Women

Two images, one a photograph of two typists being "timed" by a male supervisor (figure 40), the other, a tinted photograph of a group of *lavanderas mexicanas*, or Mexican laundresses (figure 41), are examples of how women's labor was imagined in Mexican visual culture. Although the two images are both representations of *obreras*, or female workers, they differ in a number of ways. The photograph of the typists appears to imagine clerical work as middle class, evidenced by the dress, body type, and demeanor of the models. The typists are about the same age — in their twenties or so — and wear the typical dress worn by millions of women clerical workers around the world; they sport the *flapperista*'s bobbed hairstyle and stylish high-heeled, mass-produced shoes, and they're both operating a "mechanical writer," the new typewriting machine that helped to transform the role of the secretary from a male-gendered position to a female one. The aesthetic of the composition is documentary in style, as if the photographer merely happened upon them in the midst of important work. The image infers that the typists are "busy" and that time is of the essence; the two young women ignore the camera and appear to be totally focused on their work. And, finally, the space in which they labor is characterized as modern by the furniture, the lighting, and the typewriters.

The lavanderas, on the other hand, range in age from teenagers to grandmothers. Their dress is a mixture of the traditional and the contemporary, and their long hair is worn braided according to long-established custom. They sit motionless, posed before the camera as if their work is not that important and can be suspended while their photograph is taken. Their bodies are turned to the front as they give the photographer their undivided attention, gazing directly into the camera lens. The working space is obviously not modern: the lavanderas kneel on the floor; there are no mechanical or electric machines anywhere in sight, and the washing of clothes is presented as work done by lower-class women.

Another important distinction has to do with the difference in the context of the production and circulation of each image. The photograph of the typists illustrates an article about modern office work and is addressed to a literate, middle-class Mexican audience that subscribes to one of the major weekly illustrated magazines distributed in Mexico City. The image of the laundresses, conversely, is reproduced as a postcard, intended to be circulated as a tourist travel souvenir. If the content and formal composition of the first photo are influenced by the realist aesthetic of photojournalism, this second photograph is informed by a different aesthetic, a nineteenth-century European imagination of exotic "others" that will be discussed in more detail in chapter 5. The laundresses are *tipos mexicanos* or Mexican "types," a stereotype employed by the state and the market sector as part of a projection of Mexico as a national space.

Despite aesthetic and contextual differences, both photographs acknowledge the presence of women in the public arena of economic activity and reveal the gendered nature of work. If images of domestic and fashionable women emphasize beauty, clothing, grace, maternity, and sexuality, as well as consumption, pictures of working women call attention to the fact that many women of all ages and social rank worked outside the home. Images of working women pictured the kinds of labor they

40. Modern young office women demonstrating the new typewriting machine, *Ilustrado*, 28 November 1929, 27.

J. K. 56. México. *Lavanderas Mexicanas.* "Dos semanas"
Regist.

41. A photograph of a group of Mexican laundresses, reproduced as a postcard for circulation in the tourist trade. Courtesy of Susan Toomey Frost, Uncredited hand-tinted photograph.

performed and the spaces in which they performed that labor, suggested the age and economic class of these workers, and visualized how female laborers were viewed by the culture at large. This chapter is interested in how working women were represented in visual culture. How was work gendered in these images? How did images of working women challenge or sustain dominant understandings of womanhood and femininity? In what way did representations of women at work shape the beliefs about working women in postrevolutionary Mexico?

Women and Work

During the Porfiriato, rural women labored alongside the men in agricultural fields, raised livestock, and produced crafts to sell at the local markets. Silvia Arrom notes that in the early 1800s, women "constituted almost one-third of the labor force . . . or more than one-fourth of the urban female population" in Mexico City. And Margaret Towner has determined that "by 1895 women represented approximately 33 percent of the workforce in the transformation industries [engaged in converting raw materials into manufactured commodities] and 41 percent in services, while they only represented 17 percent of the totally economically active population" (90). While this data counted seamstresses, domestic servants (the largest category), *merciantes* (proprietors of corner stores), teachers, and workers in tobacco factories, it did not consider the thousands of women who engaged in "unofficial" wage labor. This unofficial labor could have been the illegal work of prostitutes or the undeclared work done by women who took in laundry or helped out with family businesses and crafts, or indigenous women who traveled to the city daily to sell food, handicrafts, and animal products.

While unpaid domestic labor circumscribed the role of most urban women before the revolution, a significant number also engaged in outside wage labor that brought money into the family. Almost 50 percent of women in Mexico City were employed doing needlework, cigar making, domestic work, laundry, and concierge work while others were working in brothels, in dance halls, and on the street as prostitutes (Piccato, 21–29). Some stood behind counters in family businesses and large department stores, or served as teachers and midwives. The theaters and dance halls were populated with actresses, singers, and dancers while a significant number of ambitious middle-class women pursued careers in education, medicine, and dentistry.

The issue of women and work in postrevolutionary Mexico is central to recent feminist historiography. These studies look at specific case studies to illuminate the role of women in wage labor, and find that women's ability to earn wages altered their social status as well as perceptions about that status. The shift to industrial capitalism in Mexico in the nineteenth century and the increase in the numbers of women working in free wage labor had a profound effect on women's daily life, affording many the opportunity for economic and social independence. The lives of working women were shaped by, and in turn shaped, the interconnections among the various spheres and material conditions of their lives, including family, class, citizenship, and employment.[1] First, economic independence meant that a woman did not have to rely on husbands or fathers to support her and her children. Second, the transformation of work and of work spaces meant that women's access to the public sphere expanded. Third, industrialization and the introduction of new occupations for women brought significant changes to the gendering of the work space in Mexico and aggravated social concerns about working women that were linked to the idea of the separate spheres of home and work (Porter 2003, 52). For example, with the introduction of department stores and the expansion of retail outlets, more and more women found jobs as salesclerks that required them to interact on a daily basis with people outside of their own social class.

The Mexican revolution engendered significant economic as well as human losses, and by 1917 the number of workers had been reduced by more than a million and a half. Although most Mexicans — male and female — continued to work in rural-based agriculture-related industries, migration to the city and postwar changes in land ownership and industrialization increased opportunities for wage-based labor in urban areas. In 1921, approximately 75 percent of the labor force was still involved in agricultural work, 12.4 percent in industry, and only 3 percent in services. In 1930, 68 percent worked in agriculture, 12.9 in industry, and 4.6 in services. (Camín and Meyer, 123). Also, work was defined as paid employment in clearly delineated workplaces. Women's domestic labor as housewives and mothers was not understood as "work" in part because it was confined to the so-called private sphere of the home, but also because it was seen as a woman's duty.[2] As Marión de Lagos, a writer in the popular weekly magazine *Todo*, put it, "the woman has left the hearth, but has not abandoned it. She is more able to accomplish important work in the social environment, sharing with men the honors of the triumphs in work—in the air force, in art, in science—and still having time to lavish her tenderness and her attention to the home" (21 June 1935). Finally, "working women" did not always trade their labor for cash; they bartered food, as well as handmade materials such as pottery and weaving. While some worked in conventional spaces—factories, shops—others took in piecework or parlayed their goods on the street corner or in the brothel or dancehall.

While there were undeniably more opportunities for women to work outside the home in the 1920s, the census data reflects a drop in the number of employed women after the war as women were excluded from some job sectors. This drop may also be linked to the increasing emphasis on women's primary role as wife and mother as discussed in chapter 3. Additionally, the rise of the middle class and better wages for males at the expense of female wages also contributed to the decline in women's participation in the official wage labor market (Blum 2004, 70). Finally, the implementation of federal legislation addressing labor rights inadvertently affected women workers. While Article 123 of the 1917 Constitution limited the workday to eight hours, and recognized a worker's right to unionize, it prohibited women and children from engaging in certain kinds of work activities that were deemed "unsuitable" for their gender or age. According to Ann Shelby Blum, this protective legislation "pushed more women into informal sector work, especially domestic service," which generally offered lower wages and unregulated working conditions (2004, 80). She writes that in Mexico City, "women's wages were so low that it could take as many as four incomes to support a female-headed family at a minimal level of consumption" (2004, 77).

In addition to looking at changes in overall employment levels, we need to consider the shift in the nature and place of women's participation in the industrial workforce. While fewer women worked in the tobacco industry in the 1920s, the expansion of the textile and clothing industry provided more jobs for women.[3] Increasing urban industrialization and the expansion of the commercial manufacturing of mass-produced products also created a demand for more labor power. Some of the industries that hired significant numbers of women in the postwar years included those that manufactured things like matches, cardboard boxes, neckwear, perfume, thread, and umbrellas. Women also found work in the service sector, in bakeries, beauty salons, and restaurants (Porter 2003, 26–27). Of course, the effects of industrialization were complicated by class and regional differences. Susie Porter writes that in rural areas "mechanization of agricultural production provided more wage-earning opportunities for men than for women," while urban areas offered women more wage-earning opportunities doing factory work (Porter 2003, xiii).

However, the transformation of women's work cannot be solely attributed to economic pressures; changes in the social meanings of work and gender contributed to the reconfiguration of occupation and employment patterns. As discussed in chapter 3, although the Mexican revolution allowed for new kinds of political rights for women, it did not totally dispel earlier ideas about the gendered nature of private and public life. Critics representing religious and middle-class constituents condemned the entrance of women — specifically middle-class women — into the workforce, insisting that a woman's place was in the home. Discursive constructions of working women in Mexico were still tied to class, to ideals of femininity, and to the ideological distinction between public and private spheres. Jocelyn Olcott, for example, notes that national and local legislation "prohibited wives from working outside the home without their husbands' permission" (2005, 21). Regardless of the dominant discourse of domesticity, national, regional, and individual economic imperatives required that many women enter the wage-labor market. If the ideal was a two-parent household in which men worked for a wage and women took care of home and family, the reality was that in many households, men were absent, women worked for remuneration *and* took care of their home and their children, and children themselves were often officially or unofficially working for wages.

We must also recognize that many women *chose* to work outside the home for political and personal reasons. Isabel Farfán Cano, a working woman herself, interviewed a number of young women attending university in Mexico City for a 1933 article in *Todo* entitled "Why Do They Study?" One of her interviewees, Conchita Ariza, goes to school because she wants a good career so that she can be self-sufficient and economically independent from men. Moreover, she believes that all women should work to be independent. Rosita Sánchez Carrillo, who is studying for a law degree, wants to be "useful" to society in order to contribute to the betterment of women's place in Mexican culture where there still exist "many scruples and mental reservations" about women's potential. While Señorita Sánchez Carrillo plans to work, she also plans to marry, preferably a "cultivated man," if possible a lawyer. Hermilia Pérez Morena believes that marriage is not a obstacle for her professional life but also insists "woman must never forget she is a woman" (17 November, no page).

Class also shaped women's ambitions. Another female journalist, Marión de Lagos, talks to working women across different economic classes for an essay entitled "Las mujeres que trabajan nos hablan." First, she speaks with a young typist who proudly earns $100.00 pesos a month, an amount that the typist considers "very satisfactory." While this young woman supports the institution of marriage, she also believes that women need to be economically independent. De Lagos then interviews a different group of women who are attending a trade school. Some are learning to make gloves and are confident that this trade will allow them to earn enough money to support their household. Others are training to be hat makers and are certain that this will be the best career, since "no modern woman can escape the tyranny of fashion." They hope to be earning eight pesos a day when they are done with their training. Future hairdressers are confident of making three or four pesos daily (*Todo*, 21 June 1935, no page).

Visual representations of working women reveal similar class-based distinctions: lower-class women are pictured working in factories, as domestics, or selling tortillas on the street corner, while women engaged in what was deemed "professional" work — professors, doctors, and librarians, for example — were imagined as workers in very different ways, as evidenced by the discussion of the two images that introduced this chapter. On the one hand, this difference had to do with cultural conceptions about gender and class and was also related to conventionally held ideas about the kinds of work women did in exchange for money. On the other hand, these representations also challenged conservative notions of femininity and conceptualizations about the gender of work and workers. In other words, visual culture made working women and their lives visible to the community in which they labored. Images of women at work gave evidence of women's participation in the public arena of economic activity in the face of a conventional ideology that painted a picture of separate spheres. As Cathy Davidson has noted, the idea of separate, gendered spheres has never been "proven." In spite of its ideological dominance in the nineteenth and early twentieth centuries, the material reality of women's lives refused this simplistic division.

By the end of the nineteenth century, industrial labor in Mexico was divided according to gender, and work spaces themselves had become gendered. Of course, this was true for many industrializing nations due, in part, to discourses around what constituted "women's work" and to cultural understandings about the relation between gender and technology. In Kenneth Lipartito's study of the history of women telephone operators in the telephone industry, he finds that mechanization "often preserved patriarchal labor relations" in terms of the type of work women and men were assigned as well as wage differentials (1077). Telephone companies such as AT&T, for example, had employed women as telephone operators almost exclusively since the 1880s because male managers believed that women "possessed the inherent qualities needed in a manual system and that they were available in large numbers" (Lipartito, 1082).[4] Thus, it was not merely that women could be hired for lower wages that gendered the job of being a telephone operator as female; it was the imagining of this kind of labor as a "woman's job." Photographs such as that in figure 42, which shows "one hundred and fifty young telefonistas" (and not a single man) working in La Empresa Ericsson in Mexico City reinforced this belief. The representation of these workers makes the job a decidedly feminine occupation. The seemingly endless row of female figures genders the space of production as female: their seated pose denies any aspect of "manual labor" that might endanger these women's biologically "weak" bodies.

In Mexico, as in other national contexts, the gendering of the work space was shaped by particular sociocultural conceptions about femininity. For example, cigarette companies such as El Buen Tono employed women because, in Mexico, cigarette manufacturing was historically considered "woman's work." El Buen Tono promoted itself as a work space "that protected worker morality, which included separation of the sexes," thereby making it an acceptable space for women to work (Porter 2003, 22–23). The postcard depicting coffee sorters (figure 43) and the advertisement for the U.S. cigarette Monte Carlo (figure 44) reproduce this ideology by presenting coffee and tobacco-leaf sorting as gender-specific work. Looking at rural coffee growing, for example, Heather Fowler-Salamini finds that before the war women were assigned the job of sorting coffee beans in an otherwise male-dominated industry "because the task has always been considered an extension of domestic duties and therefore 'women's work.'" With the growth of "dry coffee mills," men took on the "skilled" work of "machinists, carpenters, and loaders," while women were hired as "sorters," work that was considered "unskilled" and thus worth less in terms of wages (1994, 27–38).[5]

Not only do these images picture coffee and tobacco sorting as women's work, the space of this labor is also gendered female. First, both spaces are imagined as work spaces occupied primarily by women. The photographs of the Mexican coffee sorters and the tobacco workers paint a picture of a feminized working space in which men do not figure at all or only peripherally. The space of this work is thus made safe for the working woman. The single male coffee sorter in the postcard is presented in a feminized position: he is the only one seated while the women are all standing. The other male figure is distinguished by his hat and by the fact that he is not engaged in manual labor; instead, he stands off to the side, observing in the role of a supervisor or foreman.

The work space of the Mexican garment workers in figures 45 and 46 is likewise feminized. Similar to Europe and the United States, clothing and textile manufacturing in Mexico was an area that quickly absorbed thousands of women as the ready-to-wear fashion market exploded around the globe. In the early 1800s textile factories principally employed men, but by the 1880s factories were hiring more and more women (Porter 2003, 10–11).[6] After the war, the number of women working as

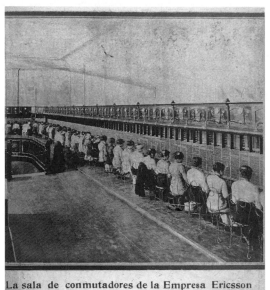

La sala de conmutadores de la Empresa Ericsson

buscar los medios de violentar los trámites que preceden a la realización de un negocio o
lo telefónico a través de cuyas complicadas redes se cruzan diariamente por término medio cien-
usas ajenas a las mismas. De el buen servicio telefónico depen de muchas veces e² arreglo favorable
hasta hoy la primacía la Empresa de teléfonos Ericsson, nos ha parecido dar a conocer al públi-
istas se ocupan de poner en comunicación entre sí a lo suscriptores de la importante red. Como se
antidad la ardua labor que pesa sobre las 135 señoritas telefonistas que con afán constante tra-

42. The gendered space of
women's wage labor: 135
female telephone operators
at the Ericsson Company,
La Semana Ilustrado, 27
January 1914, unpaginated.

No. 130 Iturbide Curio Store, Mexico

Mexico

Escogida del Café

43. A photograph of women sorting coffee beans on a coffee-growing
plantation," reproduced as a postcard. Courtesy of Susan Toomey Frost,
uncredited black-and-white photograph.

Labor de encujamiento
de tabacos claros.

44. Tobacco sorting presented as typical women's work, *Revista de Revista*,
4 June 1938, 4.

seamstresses doubled. In 1900, the clothing industry employed about
10,000 women; by 1936, approximately 17,000 women worked as seamstresses in Mexico City alone (Porter 2003, 35). Even though the number of women working in these factories increased, they generally were
assigned tasks with lower pay and considered "less skilled." According to
Porter, *costureras* or female seamstresses, in the ready-to-wear garment
industry "mostly worked in *prenda chica* [figure 45], the manufacturing
of smaller garments such as underwear and women's blouses, while men
where in charge of producing *prenda granda* or clothing items such as
men's suits" that involved more labor and were more difficult to produce" (2003, 32). The seamstresses are dressed conservatively; they labor in a gender-segregated environment; they do not operate big machinery but work only with their hands or with small, home sewing
machines, similar to the New Home Sewing Machine reproduced in
figure 34 in chapter 3. Regardless of the type of work or the social class
envisioned, these photographs of working women imagine them as
models of femininity: none are engaged in backbreaking manual labor,
or working with heavy machinery. The actual practice of work itself
as physical labor, in fact, is minimized. The laundresses, typists, telephone operators, and seamstresses are seated; their productive efforts are

45. The "patient" labor of clothing manufacturing, *Ilustrado*,
24 October 1929, 37.

osiureras que infatigablemente producen trajes mexicanos.

46. Young seamstresses engaged in "women's work," *Ilustrado*,
24 October 1929, 36.

absent, and instead we find these women to be exemplars of decorum in their dress and their demeanor.

As noted above, the terrain of women's work changed significantly, and women now worked in industries that had not existed before the war and those from which they had previously been excluded. Porter's table of "Women as a Percentage of the Adult Workforce" in Mexico City in 1921, indicates significant numbers of women in most of the sites of commerce listed, including the manufacturing of umbrellas, matches, and brushes, as well as laboratories, pastry shops, and beauty salons (2003, 26–28). One work space not listed on Porter's table, however, is the modern business office, another space in which the modern young woman was authorized to work. Studies of the transformation of the office in the early decades of the twentieth century find both an extreme growth in the number of clerical positions as well as a " 'takeover' of clerical positions by women" (Rotella, 51). This growth has been attributed to a number of different factors, including supply and demand, shifting organizational structures, the increased specialization of clerical jobs, the growth of other employment sectors that demanded male labor, and also the introduction of new technology — typewriters, adding machines, and so on — into the office environment. There are numerous explanations for the feminization of clerical work. For example, some suggest that employers saw women as transient workers who would leave employment for marriage or believed that women were more suited to mechanized office labor.

However, it was the introduction of the typewriter that ultimately transformed the clerical work space into a female gendered space. Certainly, if one examines images of typists that circulated globally at this time, it would be obvious that society *imagined* the typist as a woman. Rubén Gallo describes a photograph from the Casasola archive taken around 1910 in a Mexico City typing school that depicts rows of blindfolded young women sitting in front of "shiny new Olivers." According to Gallo, this image reveals that "business was booming in the Capital" under Díaz (77). Yet he ignores the fact that every single blindfolded student in this photograph — and there are at least fifty of them — is female. The only two male figures are located on the extreme left-hand

47. The female-gendered space of the modern office, *Jueves de Excelsior*, 28 June 1923, unpaginated.

side of the frame and the extreme right-hand side of the frame, and they are not typing. Gallo analyzes another photograph, a close-up of a portable Underwood typewriter taken by Tina Modotti in 1928, entitled "La technica."[7] Modotti's photo presents a close-up view of the typewriter that allows us to see a selection of keys, metal types, the ribbon cylinder and ribbon, and imprinted text on a piece of paper inserted into the typewriter. In Gallo's reading, Modotti's framing of the writing machine "stressed the relation between typewriters and industrial machines." He also recognizes the photo's omission of a single critical element: "Her photograph shows every mechanical part needed for typing, including the end result . . . but . . . omits the single non-mechanical element needed to operate the machine: the human hand" (106–7). Gallo, however, again does not acknowledge that it was most often women's hands that operated this new office machine. To be fair, Gallo is interested primarily in the typewriter's influence on "traditional forms of representation" (108). He notes, for example, that writers such as Mariano Azuela and Martín Luis Guzmán considered this new "writing machine" to be "superficially seductive but fundamentally useless" (72). However, when the typewriter arrived in Mexico at the end of the nineteenth century it was seen primarily as a piece of office equipment, not as an artistic or literary tool.[8]

Until the late nineteenth century, most secretaries and office clerks were male although studies show that more and more women were being hired in office settings. The entrance of women into the office environment had as profound an impact on corporate culture. As industry expanded and mechanized, young women entering the workforce for the first time were cheaper to hire and, because of conventional patriarchal relations that gave men social power over women, were subservient to authority. By the 1920s, women dominated the clerical field, attending secretarial schools and learning to operate not only typewriters but also calculating machines and telephones. This transformation occurred not just because women worked for lower wages or were more naturally "suited" to typing. Even before this transformation of the work space could occur, the idea of clerical work as women's work and the office space as a proper space for women had to be introduced into the cultural imaginary. This was accomplished to a significant extent through the circulation of images of office women in visual culture, especially the female typist, a modern girl who confidently maneuvered her way around the spaces of contemporary business practices.[9]

The growth of modern business practices and the introduction of modern forms of scientifically managed business organizations required an "army" of office workers and "an array of office machines to permit rapid collection, assembly, and production of information" (Strom, 18). Studies have shown that the feminization of office clerical work was determined by a number of related circumstances that included the rise in demand for workers, the increasing availability of educated women looking for work, the movement of men into higher-paying jobs, and the fact that most young women eventually left employment when they married, thus keeping the cost of labor low. Although office work paid better wages than factory or domestic jobs and was less physically demanding, in general women worked as lower-waged stenographers, typists, and telephone operators, while men were hired as bookkeepers and for administrative positions. The work women did in offices came to be understood as "woman's work," and the representation of women working in office environments reinforced this understanding.[10]

An online Web site, "The Virtual Typewriter Museum," features an illustration from a 1923 book on the early history of the typewriter, or "writing machine." The illustration depicts Christopher Latham Sholes, inventor of the first production typewriter, sitting at his typewriter in the lower-left foreground of the drawing. A line of women extends back behind him into infinity, suggesting that this writing machine would transform women's lives forever, as it did indeed. The advertisement for Oliver typewriters in figure 48 — "from the first to the latest" — naturalizes a history of the typist as female by comparing two images: one of a modern young female office worker demonstrating the newest Oliver model, the Oliver L-12, and another of her nineteenth-century forerunner typing on one of the earliest typewriting machines.

Early advertising campaigns promoted the idea of typewriters as machines for women. The IBM Archives Web site remarks that the "influence of the sewing machine division of E. Remington & Sons showed clearly" in the first mass-produced version of the typewriter. According to the site, the typewriter "was mounted on a stand similar to a sewing machine table; moreover, the carriage was returned by means of a foot-treadle, and Remington's first advertising billed the 'Typewriter' as a machine "the size of a sewing machine, and an ornament to an office, study or sitting room." The advertisement also declared that "it is certain to become indispensable in families as the sewing machine."[11] Later promotions for portable typewriters, such as one for the Remington Portatíl, emphasized the machine's appropriateness for the lady of the house. The ad for the Oliver L-12 typewriter pictured in figure 49 visibly calls attention to its elegant and classic design, through its comparison to a woman dressed in the latest fashionable European loungewear. There is nothing in this illustration, moreover, that literally or symbolically

48. A visual history
of the typist as female,
Jueves de Excelsior,
5 July 1923,
unpaginated.

49. The gendering of
the typewriter, *Excelsior*,
18 March 1924,
unpaginated.

refers to "work." Again, the absence of any signs of physical labor mark clerical work as feminine.

If the majority of representations of working women situated them within the relative safety of a gendered work space—the factory, the shop, the office, and so on—there were two kinds of woman workers that occupied the public space of the city street: the prostitute and the *vendedora*, or street vendor. Vendedoras have a long history of working in public spaces in Mexico City.[12] Even with the establishment of official municipal markets, many street vendors, both female and male, could not afford the rental rates of market stalls or taxes and fees imposed by the city. They sold their wares—garden produce, handmade pottery and textiles—on familiar street corners where their customers knew where to find them (Porter 2003, 139). The majority were from the lower class, predominately Indian or mixed-class races, and many came into the city daily or weekly from outlying areas.

Photographs of vendedoras reproduced on postcards and addressed to tourists were generally situated in picturesque contexts, sometimes reconstructed in a studio setting but most often shot in the actual space in which the work was conducted. Who were these women? Since they were not included in official surveys and national census data, the images of women selling tortillas and tomatillos are perhaps the only information we have that might answer the above question. The three *vendedoras de gorditas* in figure 50 display their goods on the cobblestones of an unnamed street. Dressed in their traditional rebozos, they are surrounded with other pieces of their lives, including handmade baskets and water jugs. Given the range of ages the three women seem to represent, they could be grandmother, daughter, and granddaughter. Why were these images of lower-class street vendors such a popular subject for photographers and painters? One answer may be that they were the most visible challenge to the notion of the ideal of separate spheres that pervaded understandings of gendered social roles and places in postrevolutionary Mexico. Female factory workers remained hidden behind the walls of the factory; seamstresses who took in piecework were safely ensconced in their homes. Vendedoras, however, plied their trade in the public sphere, supposedly the place that men inhabited when they went out to work or to participate in civic life. The other response, of course, is that it was

50. A photograph of women selling gordi-tas, reproduced as a postcard. Courtesy of Susan Toomey Frost, uncredited hand tinted photograph.

Vendedoras de gorditas.

Blake & Fiske, Gante Nº 8, Mexico. 8051

more acceptable to see lower-class *indias* at work that it was to see *las mujeres decentes* laboring in the public sphere, indicating that class played a major role in the public's perception of working women and that the majority of women who worked were already marginalized by class.

The prostitute, a vendedora of a different kind, also worked in the public sphere. The commercial sex industry in Mexico City flourished in a climate of social and political turmoil. In 1905 there were 11,554 legally registered prostitutes in Mexico City (this does not include unregistered prostitutes), a figure that equaled about 3 percent of the total population (E. Turner). After 1910, the number of prostitutes increased dramatically due to the economic and social devastation caused by war and the migration of large numbers of unskilled rural peasants to the cities in

51. The dangerous life of the theater, *Ilustrado*, 25 July 1929, 23.

search of work.[13] While prostitution in Mexico in the 1920s and '30s was condemned on moral grounds, it was accepted as a necessary social and economic practice. In 1926 the federal government introduced a new version of the "Reglamento para el ejercicio de la prostitución" (Regulations for the Practice of Prostitution) that required the "registration, inspection, and surveillance of sexually active prostitutes." The legislation was primarily aimed at reducing the spread of venereal diseases through regulation rather than eradicating prostitution itself.

Images of this working woman were significant in the discussion of women and work in Mexico from the end of the nineteenth century through the 1930s. The photograph in figure 51 appeared in a 1929 newspaper article entitled "La vida dolorosa de la farándula: Las chicas que trabajan en las carpas" (The Painful Life of the Theater World: Girls

Who Work in the Musical Theater) (*Ilustrado*, 25 July 1929, 23). Although the article refers to the young woman in the photograph as an "actress and dancer," it was assumed that those like her supplemented their meager wages acting in cabarets and bawdy theaters by working as prostitutes. In popular culture, *la fichera*, or the "dance-hall girl," was featured as a popular protagonist in Mexican literature and film, where she was portrayed with compassion as a victim of society. The 1931 film *Santa*, discussed in chapter 1, introduced the genre of the *cabaretera*, or dance-hall films, cinematic narratives about "good" women who were forced by economic imperatives to become "bad" women.[14] In many ways, these films were progressive, situating the modern "woman problem" as a social problem rather than an essential problem of femininity. The protagonist of these dance-hall films is a sympathetic character, a good woman forced into a bad life due to circumstances beyond her control. She embodied traditional notions of womanhood and sacrifice while at the same time serving the economic needs of the postrevolutionary social order.

Like many writers of his generation, Federico Gamboa, the author of the 1906 novel on which *Santa* was based, was influenced by French literary naturalism, represented by the work of Emile Zola (who coined the term *naturalism* to distinguish his style of writing from nineteenth-century Romanticism). Naturalist writers distinguished their work from Literary Realism by characterizing the genre as, above all, "scientific." Influenced by social Darwinism and scientific determinism, Zola, Guy de Maupassant, and others believed in the determinacy of heredity and environment on the formation of social identity and, rejecting the romantic notion of free will, saw individuals as products of historical circumstances.[15] These authors focused on the underclasses, situating their stories in the slums and barrios of urban cities caught up in the forward march of modernity and modern industrial capitalism. The characters of their novels were not fully developed psychological characters but specimens or types that represented classes or categories of society, molded not by their own moral or rational qualities but by these particular urban social settings into which they were inserted.

Despite *Santa*'s French influence, Gamboa's novel was unquestionably a commentary on contemporary concerns specific to an emergent Mexican modernity during the reign of Porfirio Díaz. (Gamboa allegedly based his character of Santa on an infamous Mexico City "working woman," María Villa, known as "La Chiquita," who was tried for the murder of another prostitute, "La Malagueña," in 1897.)[16] Moreno's 1931 film, made two decades after the publication of Gamboa's novel, speaks to a different audience. His *Santa* narrates the fictional journey of a young girl from her rural home to Mexico City and her entry into the economic sphere of wage labor through prostitution. This journey emulated the actual migration of Mexico's rural population to the modern city, the insertion of peasant workers into the machinery of modern commerce, the expanded penetration of women into the public economic sphere in the 1920s, and the growth of prostitution that accompanied rapid urbanization. The brothel in the 1931 film is portrayed as a modern space that functions both as a public commercial space and as a private domestic space. Business is transacted between the prostitutes and their clients, but at the same time the brothel is where the young women live: it is their home; it houses their new "family"; the madam functions as both mother and father; the prostitutes are "sisters."

Moral reformers during the Porfiriato classified prostitution as a consequence of moral degeneracy (W. French 1992, 528). Moreno's Santa, however, becomes a prostitute out of hunger, fear, desperation, and economic necessity. The film portrays prostitution as a necessary and profitable vocation. Interviews with prostitutes in the 1920s revealed that, like Santa, most had migrated to Mexico City in search of work and that, generally, their reasons for becoming prostitutes were similar: lack of education, limited work opportunities, family problems, and failed romance. One letter written to local officials by a jailed prostitute states, "we used to be factory workers and rural laborers, but factories have closed and activities in the field have stalled. We believed that 70% of us were forced to lead this life out of necessity, and only 30% chose it because of personal proclivity to vice" (quoted in Rivera-Garza, 173). Many, however, revealed that they choose prostitution because it was more lucrative than other economic opportunities available to women and often provided a degree of independence not available in other forms of employment.[17]

An article in a 1934 edition of *Todo*, entitled "Minimum Salaries: The

52. The case of *muchachas bien presentadas*, *Todo*, 27 November 1934, unpaginated.

Case of "Muchachas Bien Presentadas [Good-Looking Women]" focuses on the economics of prostitution. The writer notes that a review of newspaper employment notices reveals that while office boys are paid five pesos per month, cashiers begin at fifteen pesos per month, and skillful drivers may earn twenty pesos monthly, "attractive young women are offered only 'good tips'" (Luis F. Bustamante, 27 November 1934). The montage of photographs of prostitutes that illustrates this article, however, has little to say about job requirements or actual labor. It would be impossible to read these women definitively as prostitutes outside of the context of the article, which frames the women within a convergence of sex and money. The photos could easily be pictures of a group of friends enjoying a drink at the cantina. For example, in figure 52 (above), the photograph frames a young woman in front of a cloth-covered table covered with beer bottles and glasses, and she gazes assertively at the lens. A second photo in the article reveals a young woman surrounded by two men, one of whom holds a beer bottle up to her mouth. In a third, four women sit around a table with two men. While some of the women look directly at the photographer, one pulls her jacket up to hide her face. Neither of the two men seems to be aware of the camera. At most, the women in the photos could be accused of creating a spectacle of their bodies through their dress and manner. Yet, by occupying the public space of the cantina, they also appear to freely assert their status as modern women.

The images of working women discussed in this chapter reveal the ways in which visual culture contained women within traditional notions of femininity *and* celebrated modern ideals of independence and self-determination. Even if "new" understandings of gender replicated many of the "old" understandings about women and work, representations of working women visibly challenged these understandings simply by picturing women at work. At the very least, images of working women must necessarily picture them as participants in the economic field of money and labor, revealing how women were actively involved in the feminization of public space. Finally, it is essential to keep in mind that working women did not work all the time: they also had family lives and participated in other social and cultural activities. They cleaned their houses, shopped, went to the movies, attended church, and took part in political movements. Thus, when we use the term *working women*, we need to acknowledge the fullness of women's everyday life, and the fact that working was but one part of this life, something the images of work do not disclose.

Chapter 5

La Moda Mexicana: Exotic Women

The exotic as such does not exist — it is the product
of a process of exoticization. — PETER MASON, *Infelicities:
Representations of the Exotic*, 147

The "wide shoulders and slender hips" look popularized by Greta Garbo
and Joan Crawford, discussed in chapter 2, were not the only chic models available for Mexican women to adopt as a fashion identity. Other
types of female images linked to official national discourses promoting a
postrevolutionary commercial nationalism competed for their attention.
The photograph in figure 53, accompanying an article entitled "For the
Creation of a Pretty Mexican Fashion" in the weekly illustrated magazine
Ilustrado, explicitly portrays this rivalry. The group of young *flapperistas*
on top, dressed in modern ready-to-wear copies of French and American
couture that were found in department stores around the world and
revealed bare arms and legs and French cloche hats perch on their short
hair, embody the spirit of modern, transnational femininity. The bottom

53. International fashions compete with beautiful Mexican fashions,
Ilustrado, 19 September 1929, 32.

group models an alternative fashion option: that of a national style, or
"la moda Mexicana," a domestic brand of exotic femininity based on
traditional clothing of Mexico's indigenous cultures.

Beginning in the late nineteenth century, society women all over Mexico adapted the wearing of *trajes*, or folkloric costumes, as a fashion
statement. By the 1920s, well-known Mexican celebrities and cosmopolitan women were dressing up in "the *charro*'s sombrero, the beggar's
huaraches, the petticoats and shawl of the *china poblana*" (Debroise,
118). The painter Frida Kahlo and the film actress Lupe Velez, as well as
fashionable women of the social elite, appeared in the exotic dress of *la*

54. Señora Loló C. de Rivera Baz
models the costume of *la charra*,
Jueves de Excelsior, 16 August
1923, unpaginated.

china poblana or La Tehuana on the society pages of newspapers (both of these "types" will be discussed in detail later in the chapter), and in national and regional beauty contests. Señora Loló C. de Rivera Baz in the photograph in figure 54 models one traje style: an elaborately embroidered blouse, colorful skirt, wide-brimmed straw hat, and handwoven rebozo, or shawl.

The traje-adorned female character also emerged as a major star in the new Mexican film industry. Films such as *El caporal* (Juan Canals de Homs and Rafael Bermúdez Zataraín, screenplay by Contreras Torres, 1921), *En la hacienda* (Ernesto Vollrath, 1921), and *La raza azteca* (Miguel Contreras Torres, 1922) anticipated the emergence of what was to become Mexican cinema's most popular genre in the Golden Age, the *comedia ranchera*. This genre constructed an imaginary and idealized image of life on the hacienda. This celebration of indigenous influence also generated a backlash, however. In 1934, a writer for the weekly magazine *Todo* complained that according to Mexican films such as *El Anónimo* (de Fuentes, 1932), *Sagrario* (R. Peón, 1933), *Profanación*

(C. Ureta, 1933), and *Una vida por otra* (J. Auer, 1932), the nation is a "country of cowboy dandies, peasant girls wearing colorful shawls, combs, castanets." He accused filmmakers of pandering to foreign impressions of Mexico by perpetuating existing stereotypes. On the other hand, he praises *La Calandria* (R. Delgado, 1933), *Santa* (A. Moreno, 1931), and *El Tigre de Yautepec* (de Fuentes, 1933) for arriving at the "profundity of Mexican reality." While not explaining precisely what it was that made these last three films more "realistic," it appears that contemporary dress style was a fundamental quality of modernity for the author and that the promotion of exotic fashion was a form of self-stereotyping.

This chapter considers Mexico's own kind of exotic femininity through an examination of female character types that were projected to domestic and international audiences through film and popular literature, as well as through commerce and tourism. Isabel Santaolalla defines exoticism as a commodity in which "an agency appropriates a 'colonized,' domesticated version of an Other to meet its own needs" (2000a, 10). The result is not an authentic representation of the other but an "aestheticized" construction that might be read either as a desire for the other or a desire to escape from the self into something or someone else (2000a, 22). Most studies of the exotic focus on the ethnographic construction of colonized peoples by European imperial and colonial operations. At the same time, little attention as been paid to the production of a domestic exoticism that serves the intertwined interests of nationalism and of commerce. In the 1920s and '30s the Mexican state, with the help of Mexican intellectuals and business entrepreneurs, developed their own version of a "national" exotic that was shaped by Euro-American visions of Mexico and by national discourses that were central to postrevolutionary national identity, or *mexicanidad*, discussed in chapter 1.

The invocation of these increasingly familiar images appealed to Mexicans' identification with modern nationalistic icons and symbols reproduced in state-sponsored art and cinema. In addition, commercial industries appropriated images of exotic femininity to sell commercial products "made in Mexico," such as cigarettes, beer, tequila, medicinal salves, and toothpaste. In an advertisement for a Mexican beer produced by the Compañía Cervecera, for example, a diverse group of people

55. The use of exotic femininity to promote a national Mexican drink, Tequila Victoria, *Revista de Revistas*, 2 September 1923, 25.

La Bebida Popular

La enorme aceptación que ha tenido en los hogares de toda la República el "TEQUILA VICTORIA" demuestra que el público ha estimado su exquisito sabor

dance around a bottle of "the beer preferred by an intelligent public." Mixed in among fashionably attired men and woman are characters dressed up in various Mexican trajes—including *el charro* (a kind of Mexican cowboy who functioned as a symbolic figure of Hispanic masculinity) and his female counterpart, *la china poblana*, and *La Tehuana*, a Zapotec woman from the area south of Oaxaca known as the Isthmus (*Revista de Revista*, 2 September 1923, 75). An ad for Tequila Victoria (figure 55) repeats motifs found in indigenous craftwork and contemporary murals and paintings. A rebozo-wrapped china poblana is framed by the silhouette of another iconic symbol of Mexico—the cactus, a plant from which tequila, the "national drink" of Mexico, is made. The flower-like shapes in the foreground are copied from the embroidered borders of women's *huipiles*—handmade cotton blouses—and from other traditional textile weavings.

La china poblana was one of the more popular and long-lived images of domestic exoticism. Her origins are unclear, but descriptions can be found in nineteenth-century travel writing. They are present, as well, in early folkloric and mythic narratives from the seventeenth and eighteenth centuries. One historical account tells the story of an Asian girl who visited the town of Puebla in the seventeenth century, while others suggest that the costume was carried into Mexico by an Indian princess brought to New Spain by pirates. During the colonial period in the eighteenth century, la china poblana referred to a woman of "the servant class, the working-class mestiza" (Randall, 52). In her published memoir of her travels in Mexico in the mid-1800s, Fanny Calderón, the wife of a Spanish ambassador, provides a colorful description of the dress of a Pueblan woman: "A white muslin chemise, trimmed with lace round the skirt, neck, and sleeves, which are plaited neatly; a petticoat shorter than the chemise, and divided into two colours, the lower part made generally of a scarlet and black stuff, a manufacture of the country, and the upper part of yellow satin, with a satin vest of some bright colour, and covered with gold or silver, open in front, and turned back."

As Kimberly Randall had noted, the precise meaning of *la china poblana* shifted over time. By the nineteenth century, the term *china* referred to "a woman of Chinese or Asian descent . . . [but it could] also mean maid or servant girl." Other evidence indicates that "the meaning of poblana . . . simply describes a person from the village of Puebla," a town located southeast of Mexico City (53). During the first few decades of the twentieth century, la china poblana represented a particular local fashion style popular with celebrities and society ladies, and her image was appropriated to sell toothpaste, sewing machines, medicines, and Simmons mattresses. In the 1930s, la china poblana became a movie star through her central role in state-sponsored films such as *Redes* (F. Zinnemann and E. Gómez Muriel, 1934) and *¡Vámanos con Pancho Villa!* (F. de Fuentes, 1935). She also appeared in *la historieta de aventuras rancheras* (comic book serials mythologizing life on the Mexican hacienda), such as *Los bandidos de Río Frío*, *Los plateados*, *Los charros del Bajíos*, and *Juan Gallardo* (Aurrecoechea and Bartra, 154). In all her manifestations, la china poblana symbolized a particular brand of exotic femininity, one that was "made in Mexico."

The visual realization of the modern domestic Mexican exotic was not "invented" by nationalistically inspired intellectuals but was adapted from existing European images of Mexican "popular types," reproduced in engravings and lithographs and presented through diverse kinds of nineteenth-century popular culture such as "Spanish lottery tickets, French tarot decks, porcelain dishes and trays, printed cloths, calendars, almanacs, posters" and in serialized publications. Similar to the popular types produced in France, Germany, and Spain, Mexican versions were, according to Oliver Debroise, representative of the lower class of indigenous groups "whose numbers and way of life were difficult to understand fully in societies on the brink of urbanization" (115–17). By looking at a number of examples of the domestic exotic, we can see how these female icons came to function as an alternative form of la chica moderna in political and popular culture.

As the quote that introduces this chapter insists, the "exotic" does not exist. The exotic is not a material artifact or cultural practice; it is, instead, a "way of perceiving," invented by a "process . . . [that] . . . cannot be seen apart from a system of circulation" (Bohrer, 11). The exotic and exoticism are categories of difference that mark out places, peoples, and ideas that are unknown, forbidden, abnormal, pathological, or excluded. *Exotic* refers to people, places, plants, animals, and ideas. While its meaning incorporates an understanding of the idea of "foreign," it also connotes something as alien, unusual, wondrous, or malevolent. The process of exoticization visualizes these ideological concepts through aesthetic and cultural conventions of representation in high art and popular culture.

According to Frederick N. Bohrer, while the exotic may refer to a historical place or people, in practice, the exotic and exotic artifacts are only "about themselves and the Western societies in which they circulate" (20–21). The twentieth-century understanding of exoticism was a "product of the nineteenth-century consolidation of anthropology, archaeology and sociology into scientific disciplines that structured the description of unfamiliar worlds" (Douthwaite, 9). In the wake of European colonialism, professional and amateur explorers traveled through the East, the Middle East, Africa, and Latin America, encountering people and cultures they perceived as radically different from their own. They documented their encounters in diaries and scientific papers, but also visually through drawings and the new technology of photography that provided Westerners with an iconography of human types differentiated by skin color, body type, facial features, and clothing.

The scientific discourse of exoticism extended out into the popular in the form of travel writing, tourist promotion, public displays such as museum exhibitions and world fairs and expositions, national celebrations, advertising, and motion pictures. Exotic types were reproduced in engravings and lithographs and presented through diverse forms of nineteenth-century popular culture. Anthropologists brought indigenous people back to cities such as London and Boston to photograph them in studio settings that were designed to re-create actual "native" habitats. National and international exhibitions provided another venue in which to display specimens of exotic others, offering up " 'ethnological' exhibitions, representations of 'exotic' cultures," in reconstructions of their "native" habitats. Institutional and aesthetic practices of European and North American photography and those of ethnography were joined together to produce a representation of an other that took place within and sustained what Allan Sekula calls "a social and moral hierarchy" (1986, 10).

Both ethnography and photography were shaped by biological and physiological racial paradigms that argued that cultural, social, and psychological differences could be perceived on the body (Sekula 1986, 10–12). Scientific ideology combined with aesthetic conventions to produce a genre of photography that came to have market appeal. Anthropological classifications of the primitive, the uncivilized, and the wondrous were adopted by popular culture to signify exotic people, places, and fashion. Photographers appropriated the small format of the popular *tarjetas de visita* (calling cards) to present to the "civilized" world "the representation of human curiosities and types." Postcard-size images were marketed to and collected by a modern, European culture fascinated with images of "primitive" peoples (Poole 1997, 115). The introduction of small portable cameras at the end of the nineteenth century, the invention of new film-developing processes, and the introduction of paper-based photographic film and the Eastman Kodak roll-film camera made photographing in the field much easier. These photographs were then reproduced as engravings for inclusion in magazines and newspapers.

Euro-American professional photographers set up shop in the Indian, African, and Latin American continents at the end of the nineteenth century and influenced native photographers and the development of national styles of photography that identified and communicated picturesque national types. In Mexico, the Indian served as the exemplar of the domestic exotic.

The domestic exotic was identified through body type, facial characteristics, pose, and costume; rarely was she seen working or engaged in any other kind of social activity. While cultural items such as clothing baskets or looms might be included in the photograph to authenticate the subject's "Indianness," these reproductions of exotic types never acknowledged the racial and cultural diversity of the indigenous population groups of Mexico, many of whom, even by the 1920s, did not conceive of a relationship to each other or to the Mexican state (Stepan, 145).[1]

One of the earliest surviving negatives of a Mexican Indian woman was taken by a Frenchman, Paul-Emile Miot (1827–1900) in the port of Veracruz, Mexico (reprinted in Debroise, 114). It is a photograph of an anonymous woman, identified only as a "Mexican Indian." She is posed naked from the waist up, sitting on a bench on a deserted street. Her nakedness — and the fact that she is nameless — immediately defines her as an other: European and North American women did not sit for their portraits unclothed in public places unless they were paid models posing for one of the thousands of erotic photographs that were in circulation at the turn of the century.

The German-born photographer Hugo Brehme and the North American photographer, Charles B. Waite, opened studios in Mexico City, producing portraits for well-to-do families and dignitaries and supplying a booming postcard industry with thousands of images of the Mexican exotic. According to John Mraz, foreign photographers adopted a picturesque aesthetic, believing that an "idyllic, bucolic, and exotic perspective was the proper way to represent Mexico" (2001, 10). Mraz defines the Mexican picturesque as an "orientalist" project that depicts "charros sitting under wide, flat sombreros. . . . and women draped in dark rebozos." In contrast, he describes antipicturesque photography as that which "resisted the appeal of the exotic" (2001, 2–4). The picturesque image in figure 56 of *la china poblana* and her dancing partner, *el charro*, is one of thousands taken by Brehme and is representative of the North

56. Photograph of *la china* and *el charro* performing the "Mexican Hat Dance," reproduced as a postcard. Courtesy of Susan Toomey Frost, original photograph credited to Hugo Brehme.

American and European vision of Mexico as a country populated by Indians, cowboys, and peasant girls dressed in colorful clothing.

As noted earlier in the chapter, nationalist projects adopted visual and aesthetic conventions imported into Mexico by foreign travelers and artists and transformed these images and types into national self-portraits. As suggested above, the most popular "type" was the Indian (figure 57), who was appropriated as the object of *indigenismo*, an ideology that argued that the roots of modern Mexican identity could be found in its Indian culture. Indigenismo was a pan–Latin American movement that expressed itself according to sociohistorical specificities. Poole describes Latin American indigenismo as the "formation of a racial imaginary in which it was possible to conceive of the Indian as at once distant and inferior, degenerate and noble, viscerally 'other' and

57 Photograph of a "typical" indigenous Mexican woman, reproduced as a postcard. Courtesy of Susan Toomey Frost, uncredited photograph.

sentimentally 'ours'" (1997, 40). Mexican indigenismo—formulated by a Mexican elite that included politicians, intellectuals, artists, and anthropologists—argued that while the "true" identity of the Mexican was mestizo, the roots of that identity could be found in its pre-Conquest Indian culture. Manuel Gamio (1883–1960), a Mexican anthropologist who trained with Franz Boas, the "father" of modern anthropology, wrote what some consider a founding text for postrevolutionary nation-building, *Forjando patria* (Forging a Nation, 1916). In that book, Gamio argued that the Latin American Creole elite had systematically ignored the Indian. The fieldwork of Gamio and other Mexican anthropologists in pre-Columbian Indian sites, allegedly provided scientific authenticity to the ideology of indigenismo.

Another historical discourse that shaped indigenismo was the Mexican eugenics movement that gathered momentum during the Porfiriato. Like other Latin American countries, Mexican eugenicists were well read in European literature that viewed miscegenation as the leading cause of racial degeneration.[2] Despite shared assumptions, however, factors specific to historical and social contexts shaped the promotion and practice of eugenics in Mexico. Anglo-European views on racial hybridization caused uncertainty for Mexican eugenicists. Like most Latin American countries, Mexico's population had been racially mixed since the Spanish Conquest of the sixteenth century.[3] Race as a signifier of breeding or blood was subsequently used to differentiate among criollos, Indians, and Mexicans of "mixed" blood. Between 1810 and 1940, racial categories were continually modified to reflect changing notions about what constituted "racial difference." After the 1921 Mexican Census, subsequent censuses "disregarded this emotionally-loaded category in favor of providing social and economic data from which anyone can attempt to work out his own system" (Cline, 89). From 1921 to 1940, Mexico promoted a number of different and often conflicting racial ideologies, and the division between Indians and non-Indians shifted according to changing political objectives (Cline, 92).

A specifically Mexican theory of eugenics was most forcefully articulated through José Vasconcelos's essay "The Cosmic Race." Vasconcelos and other intellectuals privileged the mestizo as the exemplary of the "cosmic race" and imagined a near future moment in which the Mexican Indian would be whitened through race mixing. Vasconcelos wrote of the coming of a new age, wherein a fusion of races and classes in Latin America would culminate in the creation of a mestizo race, or what he called the cosmic race. While proclaiming to celebrate Mexican's racial mixture, Vasconcelos's thesis insisted that this new race would emerge as a result of a "cleansing" of indigenous blood through intermarriage. His ideology of "fusion" (shared by many of his contemporaries) was thus actually a thinly disguised conviction that Mexico's pre-Colombian roots should and would eventually be whitened into extinction. It was, in essence, a thesis of spiritual eugenics or, what Nancy Leys Stepan calls "constructive miscegenation" (147).

Vasconcelos's ideology served the overarching thesis of the postrevolutionary project which, as many scholars have argued, was to integrate the Indian into the nation, in spite of his supposedly racial inferiority.[4] Scholars of Mexican muralism and other styles of national artistic practices have demonstrated how Vasconcelos's thesis was realized in the work of the muralists — Diego Rivera, David Siqueiros, and Jose Clemente Orozco, among others — who incorporated iconographic Indian figures to connect pre-Columbian history to the contemporary revolutionary moment.[5] These Mexican artists borrowed from eighteenth- and nineteenth-century European images of Mexican "popular types" (Meléndez, 19). Indigenous people were painted and photographed wearing clothing defined as "typical" or "native" and displayed in a studio setting that was promoted as reflective of an authentic indigenous environment. In figure 58, an aesthetic theme of lush, tropical flowers embellishes the dress of the Tehuana as well as the bowl she carries on her head. Posed against a background decorated with more tropical plants and populated by other indigenous females, the photographic image reproduces dominant ideas about indigenous authenticity.

The exoticization of Mexico in the 1920s was also influenced by North American and European intellectual and artistic fascination with that country in the decades following the Mexican revolution. Some came as tourists, while others chose to live in Mexico.[6] The British writer D. H. Lawrence visited Mexico in 1923, and the American photographers Edward Weston and Tina Modotti lived in Mexico during the 1920s. The American expatriate Frances Toor, who first visited in 1922, settled in Mexico City and eventually published *Mexican Folkways* (1928–33), an illustrated magazine in English and Spanish that was addressed primarily to a North American audience in Mexico. The magazine included articles on art, music, and anthropology and included photographs by Modotti and illustration and reprints of work by Diego Rivera, who also served as the art editor (Delpar, 62). In the October/December 1932 issue, Toor responded to a query from the editors of a U.S. publication, the *Southwest Review*, who asked her to summarize the intentions of her magazine. Toor's lengthy response indicated that the magazine would be instrumental in "the formation of the new Mexican attitude toward the Indian by making known his customs and his art." According to Toor, the revolution made possible the discovery of "the value of the Indian just as the industrial revolution has discovered the value of the man on

58. Photograph of a "lush, tropical Tehuana," reproduced
as a postcard. Courtesy of Susan Toomey Frost, uncredited
photograph.

the street" (206). The "value" of the Indians, according to Toor, "lies in their handicrafts and folk music" (206). Her responsibility as the editor of *Mexican Folkways* was to spread her "discovery of an art and civilization different from any that I had previously known." She promised that the magazine would focus on indigenous customs, archaeology, contemporary art, music, and "the Indian himself as part of the new social trends, thus presenting him as a complete human being" (208).

Images of indigenous people were a staple of *Mexican Folkways*. The October/November 1925 edition featured an essay on "The Apparel and Hair Dressing of the Women of Yalalag," which included photographs by the Mexican photographer Luis Márquez (1899–1978). The author of the piece, Paúl Silicio Pauer, asserts that although this village of Zapotec Indians has "already assimilated modern civilization," it has conserved "some characteristics which have been peculiar to it from time immemorial, especially with respect to women, such as their dress and manner of combing their hair" (3). The caption for one of the photos states that "the women of Yalalag are noted for their difficult and unique arrangement of the hair" (167). Another features three young women from the village of San Juan Yalalag posing in native dress for the camera (figure 59). The women in Márquez's photo face the camera straight on, in a stance that denies deliberate posing. Their presentation reflects an emerging photographic documentary aesthetic that John Tagg has defined as a "regime of truth" in which the photograph functioned as a an evidentiary document. In the context of this aesthetic — constructed through content, form, and composition — the viewer is made to understand that the photograph presents an image of reality, of "real" Yalalag women.

Nuestra Mexico, another nationalistic periodical first published in March 1932, was described by its editor, Armando Vargas de la Maza, as "a monthly magazine exclusively Mexican" whose purpose was to "express the most exalted spirit of the race and national culture." He promised that *Nuestra Mexico* would limit itself solely to that which is "truly Mexican" and would include the work of contemporary Mexican painters — including Rivera, Orozco, Roberto Montenegro — and photographers such as Manuel Alvarez Bravo and Jiménez y Márquez (1). Images of women were central to the aesthetics of the magazine. For example, the

The Apparel and hair Dressing
of the Women of Yalalag

59. Women of Yalag modeling costumes and hairstyles "from
time immemorial," *Mexican Folkways*, October/November
1925, 33.

covers of the first three issues featured Art Deco–style drawings of female figures. Four women adorned the cover of the first issue. Although
the features of all four women reflect the same Indian lineage — large,
almond-shaped eyes, wide noses, thick black hair — three were dressed in
indigenous costumes while the fourth wore the contemporary fashion of
the modern Mexican woman, reinforcing the idea that contemporary
Mexican femininity shared a visible lineage with its ancestors.

Tourism was another site in which images of the feminine exotic were
adopted to promote a particular vision of the nation. Around the world,
tourism as both a practice and an industry coincided with social and
economic modernity. Eighteenth- and nineteenth-century travel writing
produced Europe's "differentiated conceptions of itself in relation to 'the
rest of the world,'" in the words of Mary Louise Pratt. Accounts of other
geographies, people, and practices mapped a world wholly different from
the one at home.[7] Modernity accelerated productivity and "extended
both the means and modes of communication and transportation, leisure

60. "Welcome to Mexico" postcard, published by Super-Mexilina Gasoline. Courtesy of Susan Toomey Frost.

time and spatial mobility," as well as "entrepreneurs who are willing to devote their capital to the commercialization of tourism" (Wang, 18). At the same time, if tourism was essentially a modern practice, it was also a reaction to the "disenchantment" of modern life and the resultant desire to see and immerse oneself in a premodern, less stressful environment (ibid.). The growing tourist industry responded to an increasing demand for visual representations of new and exotic places and people. Since the nineteenth century, the strategy of the tourist industry had been to develop a particular kind of image "code" that highlights and amplifies certain features of a destination while avoiding other features. Vehicles of tourist promotion—such as brochures, guidebooks, postcards (figure 60, above), and advertising—required particular kinds of images that involve the "beautification, romanticization, idealization, mystification, and feminization" of a particular destination (163–65). According to Ning Wang, "there are two fundamental kinds of touristic images: paradisiacal images and totemic images." The first imagines a place of escape from the concerns of everyday life; the second represents nationally sacred or historically important attractions (Wang, 163–68). Both of these kinds of places were made available for tourists in post-revolutionary Mexico.

During the Porfiriato, the state and the business sector promoted Mexico as a tourist destination as a strategy for attracting foreign investment. The development of a national train system stimulated domestic and international tourism, and the Mexican National Railroad published a small English-language guidebook, *Tropical Tours to Toltec Towns in Mexico* in 1898. The guide's introduction quotes an earlier traveler — the explorer William H. Prescott (1796–1859), author of *History of the Conquest of Mexico* (1843) — who recalls that "journeying from the coast country to the interior, traveling some twenty leagues, the traveler finds himself rising into a purer atmosphere" (5). A more contemporary traveler — an American journalist — insists that "it is doubtful whether anywhere else in the world so short a distance of travel can display a more striking diversity of sightseeing. . . . Mexico is more foreign than Europe" (9).

Tropical Tours paints a picture of a Mexico that is both modern *and* exotic. On the one hand, the guide offers images of modern buildings and centuries-old cathedrals; the bustling avenues of Monterey and the dusty, unpaved streets of the small town of Pátzcuaro. The Mexican border town of Nuevo Laredo is "an active business town," while the northern city of Monterrey is "the 'Chicago of Mexico,' a rich and progressive city of 60,000 inhabitants. . . . Here are found the gentlest, balmiest breezes, bluest skies and one of the grandest, most picturesque outlooks that ever delighted the soul of man" (11–13). On the other hand, if the tourist desires an exotic experience, they need only travel to the nearby town of Catorce, where they may find "the customs of Mexico in their purity, unaffected by the influence of the stranger. . . . Altogether this is one of the show places of Mexico" (25). The pamphlet also contains numerous photographs that visibly integrate American tourists into the exotic place. A number of photographs have optically introduced tourists into a snapshot of the landscape or a rural scene inhabited by indigenous Mexicans. For example, one photograph entitled "On the shores of Lake Pátzcuaro" depicts two Indian women washing clothes on the banks of a river. A smaller-scale image of an American female tourist is placed on the lower-left side of the photo

(72). In another photo of a village on the shores of Lake Pátzcuaro, two children stand on a rock posing for the camera. A group of ten tourists has been inserted onto the lower part of the photograph (46). Another photograph of a group of Indians standing in front of the pre-Columbian ruins in Mitla, Oaxaca, has also been doctored to include a group of Western tourists (60).

The revolution, needless to say, had a dampening effect on Mexico's attraction as a tourist destination, as many North Americans and Europeans viewed Mexico as violent and dangerous. Both the state and the private sector, however, took part in an effort to advertise a "new" Mexico to foreign and native travelers. While the private sector was, of course, motivated by economic imperatives, Alex Saragoza argues that, for the state, tourism emerged as a piece of the nationalization project that was intent on constructing a "typical" Mexico that could be marketed to Mexicans and foreigners alike (91–92). Initially, faced with massive economic and social problems, political leaders could not devote much money or effort to revive Díaz's tourist campaign. It wasn't until 1929 that a state commission for tourism was set up under the Secretaria de Gobernación. In 1930, the federal government established the Comisión Nacional de Turismo (National Tourist Commission) and assigned it three goals: "to invite, attract and entertain foreign visitors; to study and introduce modern transportation methods and equipment throughout the country; and to establish tourist offices in U.S. and Canadian cities to arrange hotel accommodations, organize and promote tours and expedite entry" (Murphy, 82). The commission's initial campaigns appeared to be successful: 68,949 foreign and Mexican tourists traveled in Mexico in 1934. After the formation of the Mexican Tourist Association in 1940, with offices located in the United States, that figure jumped to 133,209, and in total that year, tourists spent approximately 12 million pesos on transportation, lodging, food and drink, excursions, purchases, and entertainment (*El turismo norteamericano en México*, 42). Foreign tourists included businessmen interested in expanding their domestic markets and a growing middle class of Americans with more leisure time and disposable income.

The private sector recognized the growing cultural interest in Mexican art, indigenous culture, and history on the part of a certain segment of

Europeans and North Americans. Postrevolutionary Mexican art movements gained recognition in major art centers such as London, Paris, and
New York. A number of artists and intellectuals, among them Katherine
Anne Porter, John Reed, Carleton Beals, John Dos Passos, Frank Tan-
nenbaum, Will Rogers, and Dorothy Day, wrote about their infatuation
with Mexico. The writings of other travelers to Mexico — including cultural ambassadors, businessmen, and adventurers — published in guidebooks and memoirs, portrayed an exotic Mexico that was emphatically
different from the United States and Europe. Anita Brenner, the daughter of a Russian father and an American mother, lived in Mexico from her
birth in 1909 until the revolution. She published *Your Mexican Holiday:
A Modern Guide* in 1932. Brenner describes Mexico as "a slice of Europe,
a slice of the ancient east, southsea glamour, and a breath of modern
important, new-word doings in art. Sum total: a land utterly diverse
from your own" (19). In 1937 Bernice I. Goodspeed, an American living
in Mexico, published a book, written in English for a North American
readership and published by a Mexican press, called *Mexican Tales: A
Compilation of Mexican Stories and Legends*. In her preface, Goodspeed
tells the reader that she wrote the book out of a "desire to stimulate such
an interest in the history and the legends of Mexico that all who read
these stories will come to visit these scenes." She advises that "Mexico
should be the setting for your next vacation. This land . . . is fast becoming the WORLD'S VACATION LAND" (9).

Archaeological sites and folkloric costumes and customs constructed
an exotic Mexico that was promoted through guidebooks, postcards,
and world fairs and exhibitions. *Terry's Guide to Mexico*, by T. Philip
Terry, was first published in 1909 through the Houghton Mifflin Company in Boston. The 1929 edition featured an ad for "All-Expense
Cruises to Mexico: The Land of Romance and Beauty." The promotional
text declared that "everyone is talking about this enchanting country
with its mysterious Indian remains, picturesque Spanish ruins, gay modern capital and smart resort life!" (inside back cover). *Modern Mexico /
México Moderno*, a magazine produced by the Mexican Chamber of
Commerce of the United States, Inc., advertised that its purpose was "to
foster commercial and cultural relations between the United States and

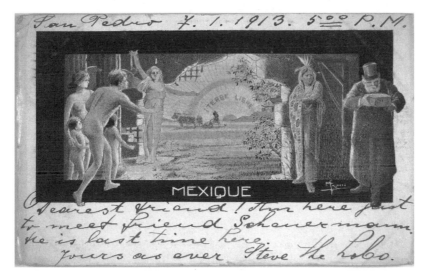

61. Early French postcard picturing the "Free Land" of Mexico. Courtesy of Susan Toomey Frost, uncredited.

Mexico." An article in the March 1931 issue, entitled "On To Mexico!" promises that a "newer and finer conquest awaits the sympathetic tourist" (6).

Brehme, Waite, and other Mexican and foreign photographers provided images for these guidebooks, and their photographs were often reproduced as postcards for local and international markets. Since the nineteenth century, there had been a big market in Europe for postcards depicting "local color" that served as souvenirs of travel and that could be sent home to family and friends. Early postcards "traveled in a circular fashion"; photographs shot by American and European photographers traveling the world were bought up by printing houses that turned them into postcards; the postcards were then shipped back to the location of photographic origin and distributed to retail merchants who in turn sold them to Western tourists to mail to friends or take home as souvenirs (Geary and Webb, 1–2). The postcard in figure 61 (above), sent in 1913 in the midst of the military phase of the revolution, appears to be have been produced by a French company, purchased in Mexico, and sent to an English-speaking friend by a man named "Steve the Hobo," whose first language does not seem to be English. Hand-drawn images appear to construct a mythical history of the "white man's" discovery of a vast and abundant new land. A female statue invites an Adam-and-Eve-like family to leave the dark "old-world" behind and enter into the bright "new world." On the right side of the drawing, a stoic indigenous figure watches a European man who is guarding a mysterious box.

The appearance of the postcard industry, an outgrowth of eighteenth- and nineteenth-colonial projects, was made possible by the development of mass-printing techniques at the end of the nineteenth century, changes in international postal regulations, and the improvement of photographic techniques.[8] Postcards quickly became an advertising staple of the tourist industry while postcard businesses arose promoting postcards in their own right that pictured landscapes, natural disasters, and special occasions (Woody, 13–16). A "picture postcard craze" emerged in Europe and the United States. People began collecting postcards and forming picture postcard clubs; a number of international exhibitions were staged in Europe (Staff, 59). Whether carried home or sent from abroad, the postcard souvenir contributed to a popular understanding of "exotic" places, people, and cultures and images of "exotic" women supplied a ready-made symbol of another world.[9] As a function of the tourist trade, the subjects of the postcard reflect the fact that the postcard was primarily a commercial item to be consumed by tourists and signify that market's expectations about difference and otherness.

Postcard collecting was popular in Mexico as well, where postcards were distributed in stores that catered to tourists in Mexico City and other urban areas. In addition to containing painted illustrations and verses written by the poet Manuel Acuña, postcards were found by photographers working in Mexico to be "an important medium for the diffusion of their work" (Montellano, 22). Waite was one of the most prolific photographers, and many of his photographs of indigenous women and children — the *tipos mexicanos* discussed in the previous chapter, — were printed and distributed by companies such as La Sonora News, Co., and the American Stamp Works (Montellano, 27).[10] While postcards offered photographers a new form of profitable commercial venues, they also provoked condemnation among cultural critics and sometimes resulted in problems with the Mexican postal authorities.

62. "Maximum" postcard of three Tehuana women that includes two stamps, which themselves contain the image of a Tehuana. Courtesy of Susan Toomey Frost, photograph credited to Luis Márquez.

Waite, for example, was incarcerated in the Belén jail for a few days, accused of circulating pornographic postcards (Montellano, 28). According to one critic, these images were indicative of the disregard foreigners had for Mexico. He writes that Waite and others "search for hidden elements and individuals that are the most ridiculous, the most degenerate, and the most miserable, exhibiting them in a state of culture-lessness and savagery" (quoted in Montellano, 28).

The type that was most often represented in Mexican postcards was *una india*, an Indian woman. Through the depiction of women "in costume," postcards in Mexico contributed to the exoticization of indigenous peoples and the "gendering of type" (Poole, 2004). The postcard industry's construction of gendered types was produced through particular strategies of representation that included shooting styles, the use of controlled studio spaces, and model poses and dress. A number of Brehme's photos of women wearing trajes circulated widely as postcards. In the example of a Brehme "maximum" postcard in figure 62 (above), three Tehuana women are posed next to an antique Spanish chest. Maximum cards, a popular collector's item in the 1920s, were a type of postcard in which the card's image — whether a photograph or a drawing — and the stamp were linked by a common motif or design. In an essay on early maximum cards in Mexico, Susan Toomey Frost describes a practice by which a "creative collector tried to find a postcard that matched the image on a stamp as closely as possible and then placed the stamp on the face of the card." In figure 62 (page 149), the image of a Tehuana figure on the two stamps pasted onto the chest reproduces the two Tehuana in the photograph.

Exotic Fashion

In Mexico, as in Europe and the United States, the label of exotic was also utilized to advertise fashion, cosmetics, and particular "looks" that were made available for women to adopt as their own in the creation of modern identities. Stylized forms of cultural referencing promoted the expansion of a commercial beauty industry that included exoticism as simply one fashion type among many available for purchase. Existing symbols of cultural, national, and racial differences were aestheticized by designers and advertisers and marketed to consumers through a discourse of luxury and style. Women wore "'Oriental' perfumes and cosmetics, 'slave' bracelets and 'barbaric jewelry,' turbans and other 'exotic' accoutrements" (Steele, 233). The French fashion designer Paul Poiret was well known for incorporating Egyptian, Asian, and European folk influences into his designs.

Cosmetics offered women an array of so-called exotic looks from which to choose. Nineteenth-century cosmetics manufacturers classified and promoted female beauty types through exotic iconographic characters, such as "American Indian, Egyptian, Turkish, and Japanese enchantresses" (Peiss 1998, 146).[11] Max Factor employed the Mexican actors Lupe Vélez and Ramón Navarro in the promotion of "Society Makeup" to Southern California Latinas (148–49). An ad for "Crema Hinds" that appeared in *Ilustrado* featured the Mexican film star Lupe Vélez wearing nothing but a Spanish shawl and high-heeled shoes (figure 63). Vélez attests that "there's nothing better than Crema Hinds to conserve a

"No hay nada mejor que la Crema Hinds para conservar el cutis blanco, aterciopelado, juvenil..."

—dice LUPE VELEZ

y la conocida y apreciada estrella mexicana agrega:

"Desde los principios de mi carrera artística he venido usando la Crema Hinds para proteger mi cutis contra los rigores del clima frío de la ciudad de México y para conservarlo blanco bajo los ardientes rayos del sol de tierra caliente. No he encontrado otra crema que supere, ni siquiera que iguale, para ello, a la Crema Hinds."

Es bien sabido que las inclemencias del tiempo son las que aviejan el cutis más despiadadamente. Más de cincuenta años de uso han comprobado la eficacia de la Crema Hinds para proteger el cutis contra el daño que causan el aire y el frío, el polvo y el sol, y para conservarlo deliciosamente blanco, fresco y juvenil. Un ensayo la convencerá.

**PIDALA DONDEQUIERA QUE VENDAN
ARTICULOS DE TOCADOR**

CREMA HINDS

63. According to Lupe Veléz, there's nothing better than Crema Hinds to preserve the youthfulness of one's skin, *Ilustrado*, 13 June 1929, 6.

white complexion, velvety, young." Vélez tells her readers, "Since the beginning of my artistic career I've used Crema Hinds in order to protect my skin against the rigors of the cold climate of Mexico City and to keep it white beneath the harsh rays of the sun of the hot climate" (13 June 1929).[12] As the Vélez/Hinds advertisement demonstrates, light skin color was a mark of feminine beauty in Mexico. While historically, racial discourse in Mexico proved adaptable to political and cultural requirements, visual culture made the color of one's skin a defining mark of indigenismo.[13] At the same time, if *la india's* skin color was not something to be emulated, her colorful, non-Western dress habits were a fashion rage among various sectors of elite society.

Poole analyzes a postcard illustration of a Tehuana, who is defined by a caption that reads "Tehuana, Street Clothes." According to Poole, the "simple comma suggests an equivalency or interchangeability between the woman and her clothes. The woman equals her clothes; the clothes equal the woman" (2004, 67–68). However, it appears that Mexican women were able to separate the indigenous woman from her attire and wear fashion modeled on the garb of la china poblana; the Huicholes in north-central Mexico; the Purhépechas, who lived near Lake Pátzcuaro in Michoacán; and La Tehuana, who emerged as one of the most popular fashion icons for Mexican women in the 1920s and '30s. An article in *Todo* entitled "Las Tehuanas, Mujeres Almos" (Tehuana Indians, Exotic in Mexico), describes these Zapotec women as "the most exuberant women in the new world" (22 September 1936).

Howard Campbell and Susanne Green describe a set of stereotypes associated with the Tehuana that rely on body type, sexuality, and clothing. According to Campbell and Green, these stereotypes "repeat 'Wild Women' portrayals and Amazon stereotypes" that have existed in numerous mythologies for centuries (156–57). They trace the development of an "ideology of Zapotec women's power as expressed in travelers' reports, paintings, anthropological studies, feminist writings and the popular media" from the sixteenth century to the 1990s.[14] The first photographer to commercialize photographs of Isthmus women appears to have been Lorenzo Becerril, a photographer from Puebla who sold a photographic series of picturesque types, shot in natural outdoor scenes, in the 1860s. Nineteenth-century explorers described Zapotec

64. A society
woman poses for
her portrait in a
photographer's
studio in Mexico
City, *Ilustrado*,
18 July 1929, 35.

women's "extremely picturesque" dresses, "adorned heads of hair," their
"colored petticoats fringed with lace," and their gold teeth (quoted in
Campbell and Green, 163–64). During the Porfiriato, Waite, Brehme,
and other foreign photographers working in Mexico City specialized in
photographing women who posed for their portraits in the trademark
dress of the Tehuana, such as in figure 64 (Poole, 2004, 64).

In the 1920s and '30s, members of the Mexican intelligentsia paraded
themselves in public wearing the Tehuana's "colored petticoats fringed
with lace." In 1926, the American photographer Edward Weston photographed Rosa Covarrubias (the wife of the Mexican painter and writer
Miguel Covarrubias) in Tehuana dress.[15] Kahlo produced a number of
paintings of herself in Tehuana costume, such as *My Dress Hangs There*
(1933), *The Two Fridas* (1939), *What the Water Has Given Me* (1943),

65. Photograph of "My Mexican Sweethearts," reproduced as a postcard. Courtesy of Susan Toomey Frost, uncredited photograph.

and *Self-Portrait as Tehuana* (1943). Although Kahlo didn't limit herself to impersonating the Tehuana — a photograph taken in 1931 by the American photographer Imogen Cunningham features Kahlo wrapped in a Mexican shawl or rebozo, another invented indigenous tradition — La Tehuana is the indigenous figure that Kahlo most identified with.[16]

Why would a modern woman want to adapt the dress and look of a poor Indian woman? For some Mexican women, the appropriation of indigenous costume was specifically political. It has been suggested, for example, that Kahlo wore the clothing of the Tehuana as a way of politically identifying herself as part Indian. Hayden Herrera writes that Kahlo's "dressing up" served as means of expressing "an essential part of her persona . . . [that] . . . served as a stand-in for herself, a second skin never totally assimilated to the person underneath" (112). Perhaps some women chose to dress up in these colorful costumes as way of defining themselves as "different" in an act of resistance against the dictates of the capitalist market. Conversely, Rick López asserts that Mexican women adopted the *trajes* "look" because it was "culturally and politically safe and racially neutral" (2002, 301). Extricated from the bodies of indigenous women and cultural contexts, flowered dresses and multihued rebozos were stripped of political significance (figure 65, above).

Anne Hollander offers yet another explanation for the adoption of ethnic or exotic fashion, suggesting that this type of fashion satisfies aesthetic desires: "the picture the garments make on the body pleases because of its resemblance to a current pictorial ideal of shape, line, trim, texture, and movement" (1978, 314). Certainly, exotic fashions based on indigenous clothing were generally marketed on the basis of style, color, and kinds of fabric. Whatever the impulse, however, the wearing of trajes by mestiza and white women remained fashionable for over two decades in Mexico. As late as 1940, an article in *Modern Mexico* announced that "Indians are chic! They have an innate flair for right posture, striking design, becoming lines. The Park Avenue Fashion leader might well envy the tilt of their straw hats, the swing of their red zarapes" (8.4 [September], 17). In a modern world in which fashion was above all a mode of self-expression, exoticism was simply another category of style through which Mexican women could advertise their modern identity.

Conclusion

Imagining "Real" Mexican Women

The Photograph always leads the corpus I need back to the body I see.
— ROLAND BARTHES, *Camera Lucida: Reflections on Photography*, 4

Lázaro Cárdenas's election to the office of the presidency in 1934 was heralded as a return to the founding principles of the Mexican revolution. A central component of Cárdenas's "Six-Year Plan" was his promise to address the needs of workers, Indians, and women—social groups that had largely been ignored by previous postrevolutionary regimes. And women were "hopeful" that Cárdenas would continue his sponsorship of women's social, political, and economic rights that he supported as governor of Michoacán (Soto, 122). Cárdenas himself argued that "a sound basis for social revolution will not be achieved until the constitution is reformed to grant equal rights," and he actively lobbied for women's suffrage (quoted in Soto, 92). Under the tutelage of Cárdenas, women served in political positions at the state and federal levels, and they organized themselves into political movements that supported the administration's socialist agenda. A number of pan–Latin

American and Mexican women's organizations were established to address the social and economic needs of women and children, including El Frente Unico Pro-Derechos de la Mujer, El Ejército de Defensa de la Mujer, El Ateneo Mexicano de Mujeres, La Liga de Acción Femenina, La Unión de Mujeres Americanas, and La Unión Femenina Ibero-Americana. And, finally, the Cárdenas's six-year reign oversaw the expansion of women's participation in the political sphere with the formation of the feminist arm of the PNR, the Partido Feminista Revolucionario (Feminist Revolutionary Party), also called Acción Femenina (Feminine Action).

There is no doubt that women's lives were transformed by social and political processes brought about by the Mexican revolution and the ensuing national projects enacted by the state, and by women themselves who participated in these processes. At the same time, however, the preceding chapters have argued that women's lives were also radically altered by the ubiquitous and often unruly forces of popular visual culture. Along with images of happy housewives and fashionable *flapperistas*, as well as women marching for birth control and national suffrage, photographs of female criminals, beauty queens, teachers, doctors, and seamstresses circulated in magazines, newspaper, films, and promotional materials. A glance at some of these images of "real" women reveal that they were not that different from the repertoire of manufactured images discussed in the preceding chapters.

A story in the Mexican weekly *Ilustrado* about women incarcerated in a women's prison in Mexico City, features a photograph of María Elena Valladares, pictured in figure 66, who "killed her lover in the corridors of the penitentiary." Dressed like Marlene Dietrich, María Elena makes a fashion statement: she wears a pair of men's trousers; a short, buttoned jacket; and a striped tie knotted off to one side. A jaunty cap is pulled down over her forehead, hiding her hair, and a fringed scarf is wrapped loosely around her neck. Relaxed, she poses with one leg bent against a stone wall. With her hands tucked into the pockets of her trousers, she resembles a young man, waiting on a street corner for a friend or lover to appear. In another issue of *Ilustrado*, a young woman with a cloche hat perched jauntily on her bobbed hair, and a boa draped over her shoulder, smiles into the camera (figure 67). This photograph accompanies a story

Luz Gonzále[...]
[...]as las hay de t[...]
indígena que, por[...]
horizontes de la [...]
virtiéndose en as[...]
que llegó hasta el[...]
La mujer otoñal[...]

66. María Elena Valladares,
an inmate at a woman's
penitentiary, dressed like
Marlene Dietrich, *Ilustrado*,
1 February 1934, 14.

67. A photograph of a "criminal
wife," part of a love triangle,
who is accused of hiring an assassin to murder her husband,
Ilustrado, 21 , 1929, 21.

He aquí, sonriente y feliz, la esposa criminal que asesinara a su cónyuge en un
día de campo, utilizando los servicios de un asesino profesional. Lea usted esta
interesante crónica de Sepúlveda, marcando el último "triángulo" de Yanqui-
landia, el que acabará sombríamente en la horca.
Página 21

Una Reina Poblana y su Corte de Amor

68. *Reinas de poblanas*, *Jueves de Excelsior*, 21 June 1923, unpaginated.

about a woman who hired an assassin to murder her husband. She is described in the caption as a "criminal wife . . . smiling and happy."

A photo montage (figure 68) presenting participants in the Señorita Mexico Contest of 1928 features photographs of a number of modern young beauties from all over Mexico who look exactly like the images of women in the fashion ads discussed in chapter 2 (*Jueves de Excelsior*, 21 June 1923, unpaginated). Doña Amalia Solórzano de Cárdenas, the wife of the president of the republic, is often pictured in the press in stories about her work with children, Indians, and poor women. A photograph of "the young and beautiful Señora María Elena Sánchez," who has been arrested in connection with the death of a professor, reveals a portrait of the perfectly made-up face and stylish bob worn by many of the beauty competitors (*Excelsior*, 1 April 1932, no page). The essay in *Todo*, entitled "Las mujeres que trabajan nos hablan" and discussed in chapter 4, includes portraits of embroiderers, hair stylists, seamstresses, manicurists, typists, and hat makers. A photograph of a smartly dressed group of women, describing themselves as "the mothers of the school, Gertrudis Armendarez de Hidalgo" and who are protesting sex education in the schools, appears in the 30 January 1934 edition of *Todo*. What role did these "real women" described above play in the popular drama of *la chica moderna*? What was the relation between real women and the images discussed in the previous chapters? Did those "manufactured" images have any relation to beauty queens or feminist organizers?

Imagining la Chica Moderna has concentrated on the specific category of visual images addressed to women that circulated in the popular culture of a predominantly middle-class consumer. As the above examples of María Elena Valladares, the beauty contestants, and *las mujeres que trabajan* reveal, there existed multiple femininities, multiple ways of being a modern woman, multiple images of la chica moderna. And all of these images could be found in the realm of a public sphere in which women could actively take part in the project of modernity. Moreover, these varied imaginings of la chica moderna offered up both progressive and conservative discourses of femininity. Women were free to pick and choose amongst these images for an identity that worked for them within the constraints and opportunities of their social and private lives.

Prevailing scientific discourses about the body and aesthetic theories of artistic and photographic representation that circulated globally presented a range of ideologies about the modern woman. These ideologies were made visible in Mexican popular culture, a site where they could be debated, rejected, and adapted by women who were increasingly addressed as major consumers. Female consumers looked at thousands of images and engaged in a practice of sorting, assigning meaning, prioritizing, selecting, and discarding. They also worked to situate themselves into the context of these images by imagining what they might look like in a particular dress, how a new cold cream may improve their complexion, what kinds of effects enemas might have on their children's health, and how a new washing machine would afford them a few extra hours of leisure that could be filled with pleasurable activities. Some may have considered whether a new sewing machine might offer them the opportunity to bring more cash into their household or cut down on household expenses.

The visual representations of la chica moderna in Mexican popular culture evidence Mexico's attempt to deal with the challenges and uncertainty of profound social and cultural changes in the decades following the Mexican revolution. While the consumption of the visual iconography of modernity — in the form of advertising, motion pictures, and photography — should of course be situated within the specific historical condition of postrevolutionary cultural politics, because of the global systems through which visual culture was produced and circulated, this iconography must also be understood as a phenomenon linked to global notions of modern identity. At the same time, if mass culture in Mexico in the 1920s and '30s was indebted to U.S. and European discourses on modernity, Western ideologies did not simply impose themselves on postrevolutionary Mexican nationalism. Instead, Mexican women drew on those ideologies and discourses that captivated their imagination in order to participate in the fashioning of their own modern Mexican lives. A kind of push-and-pull dialectic shaped the course and form of the modern Mexican citizen: if the state actively asserted a modern national identity as the crux of the new nation, many women vigorously claimed a modern identity that was unavoidably commercial and global in nature.

Notes

Introduction

1 Of course, as Serge Gruzinski has suggested, visual images have operated historically in the "modernization" of Latin America. Gruzinski writes that since the European conquest of the Americas in the fifteenth century, "the gigantic enterprise of Westernization that swooped down upon the American continent became in part a war of images that perpetuated itself for centuries" (2–3).

2 I do not use the term *middle class* to describe a specific social class, but rather to designate an "ideology" of class that pervaded public discourse. In this sense, *middle-class* designates a "particular representation of cultural values, beliefs and practices that existed prior to, or simply apart from their eventual conceptual coalescence into a social category" (Shevelow, 10).

3 See, for example, Rita Felski, *The Gender of Modernity*; Ida Blom, "Gender and Nation in International Comparison"; and Joan Scott, *Feminism and History*.

4 Interestingly, the cover of Nira Yuval-Davis's book, *Gender and Nation*, is illustrated with a painting by the Mexican artist Frida Kahlo, *Autorretrato en la frontera entre México y los Estados Unidos*. In this painting, Kahlo — dressed in a pink, colonial-style dress — straddles the border between Mexico, repre-

sented by Aztec ruins and tropical flowers, and the United States, symbolized by skyscrapers, the Ford Motor Company, and other images of technology.

5 See, for example, Jocelyn Olcott, *Revolutionary Women in Postrevolutionary Mexico*; Mary Kay Vaughan, *Cultural Politics in Revolution*; and Julia Tuñón Pablos, *Women in Mexico*. Following Joan Scott, feminist historians acknowledge that concepts of gender are "established as an objective set of references [that] structure perception and the concrete and symbolic organization of all social life" (Scott, 45).

6 See, for example, Alan Knight, "Popular Culture and the Revolutionary State in Mexico, 1910–1940"; Anne Rubenstein, *Bad Language, Naked Ladies, and Other Threats to the Nation*; Mary Kay Vaughan, *Cultural Politics in Revolution*; and Vaughan and Stephen E. Lewis, the anthology *The Eagle and the Virgin*.

7 For another perspective on Latin American modernity, see Enrique Dussel, "Eurocentrism and Modernity." Dussel argues that Europe's "experience of discovery" of the Americas was central to European modernity and that "the immature European ego" only became "master-of-the-world" at the Conquest of Mexico (74).

8 In 1910, the literacy rate in Mexico was around 25 percent, and this was primarily in urban areas. One of the major projects of the administration of President Lázaro Cárdenas (1934–40) was the promotion of public education and national literacy campaigns with the result that "by the end of the thirties, 42 percent of the population could read and write" (Bartra, 305). See, also, Vaughan (1997).

9 In *Techniques of the Observer*, for example, Jonathan Crary shows how ways of seeing and social understandings of vision itself were reshaped through processes of modernization that involved the reformation of subjectivity.

10 See Elizabeth Grosz's *Volatile Bodies*, especially chap. 6, "The Body as Inscriptive Surface," for a discussion of the ways in which we "write" identities upon our bodies. Grosz acknowledges that while social procedures aggressively mark the body "according to the morphology and categorization of the body into socially significant groups — male and female, black and white," at the same time the body is also "incised through 'voluntary' procedures, life-styles, habits, and behaviors. . . . [These include] make-up, stilettos, bras, hair sprays, clothing" (141–42).

I. Visualizing the New Nation

1 Moreno's film was the second adaptation of Gamboa's novel. An earlier version, directed by Luis G. Peredo, was released in 1918 and also enjoyed popular and critical success.

2 See Pablo Piccato's chap. 1 in *City of Suspects* for a sustained and descriptive account of Porfirian Mexico City.

3 In fact, Roger Hansen notes that the domestic market in Mexico in 1910 was limited to "three million of Mexico's fifteen million inhabitants" (24). See also Roderic A. Camp, *Entrepreneurs and Politics in Twentieth-Century Mexico*, especially chap. 2

4 According to a study conducted by Luis Lara y Pardo, "slightly more than 15 percent of the city's young adult women were officially engaged in sex work" during the late Porfiriato. See Katherine Bliss's *Compromised Positions* (32–33).

5 See also Héctor Aguilar Camín's and Lorenzo Meyer's chap. 2, "The Revolutions are the Revolution: 1913–1920," in *In the Shadow of the Mexican Revolution*.

6 See, for example, Alan Knight, "Popular Culture and the Revolutionary State in Mexico, 1910–1940."

7 Campesinos were leaving their rural homes before the revolution due to concentration of land ownerships that forced peasants off their land. While some migrated to the United States, others traveled to Mexican cities, seeking wage labor. See William French, *A Peaceful and Working People*, for an account of a *población flotante* during the Porfiriato.

8 See Vaughan, *Cultural Politics in Revolution*, for a sustained discussion and analysis of national educational projects focused on rural communities.

9 See Paul J. Vanderwood, *Border Fury*.

10 See Ilene O'Malley, *The Myth of the Mexican Revolution*; and Thomas Benjamin, *La Revolución*, for discussions of the institutionalization of the "hero cult," through which postrevolutionary regimes elided the significant political differences among key revolutionary leaders and transformed them into "official heroes" of the revolution (O'Malley, 7).

11 See Benjamin for a sustained discussion of the construction of myth and memory around the Mexican revolution. Benjamin's argument is that "the talking, singing, drawing, painting, and writing" of postrevolutionary politicos and intellectuals "invented *la Revolución*" (14). See also O'Malley's *The Myth of the Mexican Revolution*.

12   Knight, for example, writes that ultimately, the forces of "drift" — those of private and foreign investment, urbanization, population growth, and so on — had more of an effect on popular culture than the persistent efforts of the state (1990, 252–58).

13   Camp notes that the postrevolutionary leadership took Díaz's successes and failures to heart, understanding that "the political and economic aspirations of a broad group of Mexicans must be fulfilled to maintain political stability." In fact, the communication between business and the state "increased notably after the revolution. See Camp, *Entrepreneurs and Politics in Twentieth-Century Mexico*, 15. See also Nora Hamilton, *The Limits of State Autonomy*; and Robert F. Smith, *The United States and Revolutionary Nationalism in Mexico, 1916–1932*.

14   By 1910, the United States had an investment of more than $1 billion in major Mexican industries (Hamilton, 24).

15   Stephen H. Haber has calculated that in 1895, out of a population of 12.6 million, approximately 5 million Mexicans had a high enough income to participate in a limited way as consumers in the market of manufactured goods (27).

16   T. Jackson Lears describes a "therapeutic ethos" that emerged as a function of consumer society as ideals of the protestant work ethic gave way to the valorization of a culture of leisure and individuality. See his *Fables of Abundance* (1994).

17   For discussions of the social function of advertising, see for example, Marchand, "Advertising as Social Tableaux" (2000); and Daniel Delis Hill, *Advertising to the American Woman, 1900–1999*.

18   In fact, according to Julio Moreno, Mexican advertising didn't take off until the National Secretariat of the Economy stepped in during the early 1930s "to coordinate efforts to publicize the effectiveness of advertising in increasing sales." Moreno argues that in Mexico, ultimately, "it was "government leaders" and politicians, rather than businessmen, who first "saw advertising as the driving force" of the modern Mexican economy (2003, 25).

19   See also Smith, *The United States and Revolutionary Nationalism in Mexico, 1916–1932*, chap. 6, for a discussion of the alliance between U.S. business interests and the Wilson administration with the intention of maintaining "the economic-political hegemony of the United States in the Western Hemisphere" (133).

20   Cynthia White quotes the editor of the *Lady's Magazine*, who in 1825 wrote the "women have completely abandoned all attempts to shine in the political horizon, and now seek only to exercise their virtues in domestic retirement" (39).

2. Fashioning *la Chica Moderna*

1   Mexico has a rich history of political satire that took the form of satirical illustrations in the popular press that proliferated during the second Porfiriato. See Aurrecoechea's and Bartra's two-volume *Puros cuentos*; and Rubenstein's *Bad Language, Naked Ladies, and Other Threats to the Nation*.

2   Fordism refers to a mode of production introduced by the car manufacturer Henry Ford, who developed a mode of mechanized production based on an increased division of labor, which in turn facilitated the emergence of a culture of mass consumption.

3   In her book *America's Great Illustrators*, Susan E. Meyer describes the Gibson Girl as "taller than the other women currently seen in the pages of magazines. . . . [She was] infinitely more spirited and independent, yet altogether feminine. . . . She was poised and patrician. Though always well bred, there often lurked a flash of mischief in her eyes" (217).

4   *La garçonne* was the title of a novel by French author Victor Margueritte and published in 1922 that narrated the story of a modern young French woman. For Mary Louise Roberts, "the *garçonne* functions as a symbol of postwar cultural crisis and, through her own redemption, appeases both cultural and gender anxieties" (1994, 47).

5   "William Randolph Hearst used Harrison Fisher's drawings on virtually every cover of his *Cosmopolitan* magazine from 1912 until the artist's death in 1934. Likewise, a mere glance at a John Held flapper alerted the readers of the 1920s that they were probably looking at an issue of either *Life* or *Judge* magazine" (Kitch).

6   I found reproductions of these advertisements on an online site maintained by "Tobacco Documents Online." Web pages of Tobaccodocuments.org accessed 10 September 2007; printouts on file with author.

7   Interestingly, the Mexican tobacco company El Buen Tono conceived of a historicta (comic book) as an advertising strategy to promote El Buen Tono cigarettes. The title of the historieta was *Historia de una mujer* (History of a Woman).

8   U.S. government and industry groups recognized early on that the Hollywood films could "perform a service to American business." Will Hays, president of the Motion Picture Producers and Distributors of America (MPPDA) proclaimed in an often quoted radio speech that "the motion picture carries to every American at home, and to millions of potential purchasers abroad, the visual, vivid perception of American manufactured Products" (quoted in Eckert, 104).

9 See Charles Eckert's "The Carole Lombard in Macy's Window" for a discussion of the link between the "showcasing of fashions" and the "establishment of 'tie-ups'" that defined the "story of Hollywood's plunge into the American Marketplace" (106).

10 Women were very active in journalism in the 1920s and 1930s. A number of feminist and leftist journals aimed at a women were published, including *Mujeres*, *Rebeldía*, *La Mujer*, *El Hogar*, *La Voz de la Mujer*, and *Luz*. Women journalists wrote regularly for communist newspapers and also for mainstream magazines such as *La Revista de Revistas* and *El Universal Ilustrado* (Soto, 81–81).

11 Jennifer Craik challenges the notion that fashion codes are imposed upon individuals by the forces of the market. Instead, she wants to consider women's continued fascination with fashion, the pleasures fashion provides especially for women, and the ways in which women use fashion to articulate identities (16).

3. Domesticating *la Chica Moderna*

1 The cult of domesticity was not an invention of the nineteenth century. As early as the seventeenth century, we find the gendered separation of public and private spheres in Western and non-Western societies.

2 Although advertising revenue quadrupled between 1910 and 1922, "advertising was not a high priority among Mexican businesses," until the National Secretariat of the Economy stepped in during the early 1930s "to coordinate efforts to publicize the effectiveness of advertising in increasing sales." According to Moreno, it was "government leaders" and politicians, rather than businessmen, who first "saw advertising as the driving force" of the modern Mexican economy (2003, 25).

3 According to scholars of Mexico's economic history, export industrialization (an economic model that emphasizes production for export rather than for domestic consumption) defined the period from the Porfiriato through 1929, although the "dismantling" of this economic structure of course began with the revolution (Story, 25–27). See, for example, Dale Story, *Industry, the State, and Public Policy in Mexico*; Timothy King, *Mexico: Industrialization and Trade Policies since 1940*; Haber, *Industry and Underdevelopment*; and Hansen, *The Politics of Mexican Development*.

4 See also Glenna Matthews, *"Just a Housewife."*

5 Interestingly, the goal of the academic discipline of home economics was not only to give status to housework, but also to establish opportunities for

women to work outside the home, in such fields as health and nutrition, and childhood education.

6   See also Matthews.

7   See Anne McClintock's *Imperial Leather* for a discussion of the early promotion of soap in the eighteenth century, when soap served as "an exemplary mediating form" that helped promote "emergent middle-class values" within a cult of domesticity (208). See Vinikas, chap. 5, "The Cleanliness Crusade" for a history of the soap industry in the United States.

8   Christina Hardyment notes that "the first house in the world to be completely lit by electric light was the Glasgow home of the eminent [British] scientist Lord Kelvin" in 1881, and that "by 1902, 8 per cent of American homes had mains electricity" (28).

9   The term Art Deco derives from the 1925 Paris Exposition Internationale des Arts Décoratifs et Industriels Modernes, although, as Lucy Fischer notes, the term itself was not actually introduced until the 1960s (11).

4. Picturing Working Women

1   See, for example, Susie Porter, *Working Women in Mexico City*; Ann Shelby Blum, "Cleaning the Revolutionary Household" (1998); Heather Fowler Salamini, essays on women in the coffee-growing industry (1994, 2002); and Mary Kay Vaughan, *Cultural Politics in Revolution* (1997). See also John A. French and Daniel James, "Introduction," in *The Gendered Worlds of Latin American Women Workers* (1997) for a discussion of the social changes wrought by transformations in work across Latin America in the early twentieth century.

2   Like most scholarly discussions of working women in Mexico, the discussion by Porter, in her otherwise excellent book *Working Women in Mexico City* disregards "housework" in her discussion of women and work. For a theoretical discussion of the exclusion of housework from the sphere of work see Louise A. Tilly and Joan Scott, *Women, Work, and Family*.

3   For discussions of the transformation in women's wage labor after the war, see Porter, *Working Women in Mexico City*; Fowler-Salamini, "Women Coffee Sorters Confront the Mill Owners and the Veracruz Revolutionary State, 1915–1918"; and Jocelyn Olcott, "Worthy Wives and Mothers."

4   See also Venus Green, "The Impact of Technology upon Women's Work in the Telephone Industry, 1880–1890."

5   Similarly, Michael Snodgrass has documented that even though "the proportion of female workers increased from fifteen to twenty percent during

the 1920s" at the Cuauhtémoc Brewery in the northern city of Monterrey, work was still gendered on the production lines and hiring practices favored men over women (63).

6   Ann Farnsworth-Alvear, in *Dulcinea in the Factory*, notes that "like industrialists in a variety of other world regions" textile manufacturers in Colombia imported ideas about manufacturing as well as technology from Europe. One of those ideas was the assumption that the workforce would be primarily female (14–15).

7   A reproduction of "La technica" can be found on p. 63 of Gallo's *Mexican Modernity*.

8   Looking at advertisements for typewriters in Great Britain and the United States at the end of the nineteenth century, Julia Kirk Blackwelder notes that manufacturers and promoters of the typewriter "thought of the typewriter as a literary machine, not a business machine" (23).

9   See Blackwelder, "Mop and Typewriter"; Christopher Keep, "The Cultural Work of the Type-writer Girl"; and Sharon Hartman Strom, " 'Light Manufacturing.' "

10   In their analysis of the feminization of the office in the United States between 1880 and 2000, Michael B. Katz, Mark J. Stern, and Jamie J. Fader find that "in 1910, 38 percent of bookkeepers, 85 percent of stenographers and typists, and 18 percent of clerks were women. Women became a majority of bookkeepers between 1910 and 1920 and of clerks in the 1950s" (71).

11   E. Remington and Sons emerged in the early 1800s as a weapons manufacturer and began manufacturing and distributing sewing machines in middle of the nineteenth century.

12   See Porter, chap. 6, in *Working Women in Mexico City*.

13   A few years before the release of Moreno's film, an anti-venereal-disease film produced for the state public health agency by an American production company was screened in downtown theaters for Mexican audiences. Entitled *The End of the Road*, the film depicted shocking images of bodies afflicted by untreated syphilis and gonorrhea, and suggested that prostitution was the main culprit. See Bliss, *Compromised Positions* (186).

14   See Joanne Hershfield, *Mexican Cinema, Mexican Woman: 1940–1950*, for a discussion of the *cabaretera* genre.

15   Another Mexican film about a tragic prostitute, Arcady Boytler's 1933 melodrama, *La mujer del puerto* (Woman of the Port), was in fact based on a story by Guy de Maupassant.

16   See Robert Buffington and Pablo Picatto, "Tales of Two Women."

17   See also Bliss, *Compromised Positions*, and Picatto, *City of Suspects*. Judith

Walkowitz uncovers similar statistics in her study of prostitution in nine-teenth-century England. She writes that "the limited geographic mobility of prostitutes" and the "differential concentration of prostitutes in various ur-ban areas" suggest that "women's move into prostitution was circumstan-tial, not premeditated" (22).

5. *La Moda Mexicana*: Exotic Women

1   Before the Conquest, the area now known as Mexico was populated by indigenous peoples differentiated primarily by language and cultural prac-tices. By the time of the revolution, war, famine, disease, and intermarriage had decimated this population, in some cases wiping out entire groups.

2   See Stepan's *The Hour of Eugenics* for a discussion of Latin American eu-genics movements.

3   Unlike the British colonialists of North America, who did not intermarry with the native population, the Spanish did so in great numbers. By the time of the Mexican revolution, most Mexicans could trace their ancestry to various combinations of European, Indian, and African blood.

4   In his essay "The Race Problem," Vasconcelos argued that "the Indian has no civilized standards upon which to fall back. He has no language of his own, never had a language common to all of the race" (90).

5   See, for example, Jean Charlot, *The Mexican Mural Renaissance*; and Rick López "Lo Más Mexicano de México" (2001).

6   See Helen Delpar, *The Enormous Vogue of Things Mexican* for a sustained discussion of "the evolution of cultural relations between the United States and Mexico" during this period (viii).

7   See, for example, Fanny Calderón de la Barca's, *Life in Mexico during a Residence of Two Years in That Country*, a chronicle of her travels in Mexico in the 1850s.

8   See Staff's *The Picture Postcard and Its Origins* for a history of the postcard's origins and development.

9   See Malek Alloula's *The Colonial Harem*. Alloula suggests that with the death of the Orientalist genre of painting, "photography steps in to take up the slack . . . [and] the postcard does it one better" (Alloula, 4).

10 As John Mraz notes, in "Today, Tomorrow, and Always," these picture post-cards were preceded by an earlier popular form, the *tarjetas de visita* that circulated in Mexico in the middle of the nineteenth century (116).

11 Kathy Peiss suggests that such a typology offered American women "a means

of perceiving and classifying the dizzying array of complexions in a nation of immigrants," even addressing those immigrants through specific marketing strategies (1998, 148).

12 Hinds Cream used testimonials to promote their product throughout the 1920s and 1930s. In a 1923 Hinds Cream ad photo in the February 1923 edition of *Theatre* magazine, theater actress Lenore Ulric confirms that "Hinds Crème is perfectly wonderful!"

13 Deborah Poole makes this point in her analysis of the formation of Oaxacan regional identity at the turn of the twentieth century (2004, 41).

14 Chapman and others date the origin of this myth to the mid-nineteenth century, when a Zapotec woman, "la india Teresa," killed a Spaniard during a Zapotec rebellion. See also DeMott's *Into the Hearts of the Amazons*.

15 Miguel Covarrubias's sojourn in the Isthmus of Tehuantepec in the 1940s resulted in a series of painting of Tehuana women. In 1946 he published *Mexico South: The Isthmus of Tehuantepec*, based on research he conducted in the Isthmus during that period.

16 Chloë Sayer has remarked on the difficulty of tracing the history of the rebozo. Its origins have been variously located as Aztec, Spanish, or Oriental, but Sayer claims that it most likely "represents a synthesis of various cultures." First named in the sixteenth century by the Spanish cleric Frey Diego Durán, by the eighteenth century the rebozo had become a fashion statement and versions of the rebozo were being worn by women of all social classes (106).

Bibliography

Abrams, Lynn. *The Making of Modern Woman: Europe, 1789–1918*. London. Longman, 2002.

Aguilar Camín, Héctor, and Lorenzo Meyer. *In the Shadow of the Mexican Revolution: Contemporary Mexican History, 1910–1989*. Austin: University of Texas Press, 1993.

Albiñana, Salvador, and Horacio Fernández. *Mexicana: Fotografía moderna en méxico, 1923–1940*. Valencia: Generalitat Valenciana, 1991.

Alloula, Malek. *The Colonial Harem*. translated by Myrna Godzich and Wlad Godzich. Minneapolis: University of Minnesota Press, 1986.

Amos, A., and M. Hagalund. "From Social Taboo to 'Torch of Freedom': The Marketing of Cigarettes to Women." *Tobacco Control* 9 (March 2000): 3–8.

Anderson, Benedict. *Imagined Communities: Reflections on the Origin and Spread of Nationalism*. London, Verso, 1983.

Andrews, Maggie, and Mary M. Talbot, eds. *All the World and Her Husband: Women in Twentieth-Century Consumer Culture*. London: Cassell, 2000.

Arias, Patricia. "Three Microhistories of Women's Work in Rural Mexico." In *Women of the Mexican Countryside, 1850–1990*, edited by Heather Fowler-Salamini and Mary Kay Vaughan. Tucson: University of Arizona Press, 1994.

Arrom, Silvia Marina. *The Women of Mexico City, 1790–1857*. Stanford: Stanford University Press, 1985.

Aughinbaugh, W. E. *Advertising for Trade in Latin-America*. New York: Century Company, 1922.

Aurrecoechea, Juan Manuel, and Armando Bartra. *Puros cuentos: La historia de la historieta en México, 1874–1934*. 2 vols. Mexico City: Grijalbo, 1988.

Auslander, Leona. *Taste and Power: Furnishing Modern France*. Berkeley: University of California Press, 1996.

Barnard, Malcolm. *Fashion as Communication*. London: Routledge, 1996.

Barthes, Roland. *Camera Lucida: Reflections on Photography*. New York: Hill and Wang, 1981.

———. *The Fashion System*. New York: Hill and Wang, 1983.

———. "Rhetoric of the Image." In *Image/Music/Text*, translated by Stephen Heath. New York: Hill and Wang, 1977.

Bartra, Armando. "Seduction of the Innocents." In *Everyday Forms of State Formation: Revolution and the Negotiation of Rule in Modern Mexico*, edited by Gilbert M. Joseph and Daniel Nugent. Durham, N.C.: Duke University Press, 1994.

Bauer, Arnold J. *Goods, Power, History: Latin America's Material Culture*. Cambridge: Cambridge University Press, 2001.

Beatty, Edward. "Commercial Policy in Porfirian Mexico: The Structure of Protection." In *The Mexican Economy, 1870–1930*, edited by Jeffrey L. Bortz and Stephen Haber. Stanford: Stanford University Press, 2002.

Beecher, Catherine. *The American Woman's Home: On Principles of Domestic Science*. Boston: J. B. Ford, 1869.

———. *A Treatise on Domestic Economy*. Boston: Thomas H. Webb and Company, 1842.

Beetham, Margaret. *A Magazine of Her Own? Domesticity and Desire in the Woman's Magazine, 1800–1914*. London: Routledge, 1996.

Beezley, William H. *Judas at the Jockey Club and Other Episodes of Porfirian Mexico*. 2nd ed. Lincoln: University of Nebraska Press, 2004.

Benjamin, Thomas. *La Revolución: Mexico's Great Revolution as Memory, Myth, and History*. Austin: University of Texas Press, 2000.

Benjamin, Walter. *The Arcades Project*. Cambridge, Mass.: Belknap Press of Harvard University Press, 1999.

Berger, Dina. *The Development of Mexico's Tourist Industry: Pyramids by Day, Martinis by Night*. New York: Palgrave Macmillan, 2006.

Berger, John. *Ways of Seeing*. New York: Penguin Books, 1972.

Berman, Marshall. *All That Is Solid Melts into Air: The Experience of Modernity*. London: Verso, 1983.

Berry, Sarah. *Screen Style: Fashion and Femininity in 1930s Hollywood*. Minneapolis: University of Minnesota Press, 2000.

Blackwelder, Julia Kirk. "Mop and Typewriter: Women's Work in Early Twentieth-Century Atlanta." *Atlanta History Journal* (fall 1983): 21–30.

Bliss, Katherine. *Compromised Positions: Prostitution, Public Health, and Gender Politics in Revolutionary Mexico City*. University Park: Pennsylvania State University Press, 2001.

———. "A Right to Live as *Gente Decente:* Sex Work, Family Life, and Collective Identity in Early-Twentieth-Century Mexico." *Journal of Women's History* 15.4 (2004): 164–69.

Blom, Ida. "Gender and Nation in International Comparison." In *Gendered Nations: Nationalisms and Gender Order in the Long Nineteenth Century*, edited by Ida Blom, Karen Hagemann, and Catherine Hall. New York: Berg, 2000.

Blum, Ann Shelby. "Cleaning the Revolutionary Household: Domestic Servants and Public Welfare in Mexico City, 1900–1935." *Journal of Women's History* 15.4 (winter 2004): 67–90.

———. "Public Welfare and Child Circulation: Mexico City, 1877 to 1925." *Journal of Family History*, 23.3 (July 1998): 240–72.

Bohrer, Frederick N. *Orientalism and Visual Culture: Imagining Mesopotamia in Nineteenth-Century Europe*. Cambridge: Cambridge University Press, 2003.

Bowden, Sue, and Avner Offer. "The Technological Revolution That Never Was: Gender, Class, and the Diffusion of Household Appliances in Interwar England." In *The Sex of Things: Gender and Consumption in Historical Perspective*, edited by de Grazia with Ellen Furlough. Berkeley: University of California Press, 1996.

Bortz, Jeffrey. "The Revolution, the Labour Regime, and Conditions of Work in the Cotton Textile Industry in Mexico, 1910–1927." *Journal of Latin American Studies* 32.3 (October 2000): 671–703.

Breitbart, Eric. *A World on Display: Photographs from the 1904 St. Louis World's Fair*. Albuquerque: University of New Mexico Press, 1997.

Brenner, Anita. *Your Mexican Holiday: A Modern Guide*. New York: G. P. Putnam's Sons, 1932.

Brown, Joshua. *Beyond the Lines: Pictorial Reporting, Everyday Life, and the Crisis of Gilded Age America*. Berkeley: University of California Press, 2002.

Bruzzi, Stella. *Undressing Cinema: Clothing and Identity in the Movies*. London: Routledge, 1997.

Buchenau, Jürgen. *Tools of Progress: A German Merchant Family in Mexico City, 1865–present*. Albuquerque: University of New Mexico Press, 2004.

Bucklie, Cheryl, and Hilary Fawcett. *Fashioning the Feminine: Representation and Women's Fashion from the Fin de Siècle to the Present*. London: I. B. Publishers, 2002.

Buffington, Robert, and Pablo Piccato. "Tales of Two Women: The Narrative Construal of Porfirian Reality." *Americas* 55.3 (January 1999): 391–424.

Burgin, Victor. "Looking at Photographs." In *The Photography Reader*, edited by Liz Wells. London: Routledge, 2003.

Camp, Roderic A. *Entrepreneurs and Politics in Twentieth-Century Mexico*. New York: Oxford University Press, 1989.

Campbell, Howard, and Susanne Green. "A History of Representations of Isthmus Zapotec Women." *Identities* 3.1–3.2 (1996): 155–82.

Cannon, Aubrey. "The Cultural and Historical Contexts of Fashion." In *Consuming Fashion: Adorning the Transnational Body*, Anne Brydon and Sandra Niessen. New York: Berg, 1998.

Certeau, Michel de. *The Practice of Everyday Life*. Berkeley: University of California Press, 1984.

Charlot, Jean. *The Mexican Mural Renaissance, 1920–1925*. New Haven: Yale University Press, 1963.

Cline, Howard F. *Mexico: Revolution to Evolution, 1940–1960*. New York: Oxford University Press, 1962.

Coffey, Mary K. "Angels and Prostitutes: José Clement Orozco's *Catharsis* and the Politics of Female Allegory in 1930s Mexico." *New Centennial Review* 4.2 (2004): 185–217.

Coffin, Judith G. "Credit, Consumption, and Images of Women's Desires: Selling the Sewing Machine in Late Nineteenth-Century France." *French Historical Studies* 18.3 (spring 1994): 749–83.

Coffman, Elisabeth. "Women in Motion: Loie Fuller and the 'Interpenetration' of Art and Science." *Camera Obscura* 17.1 (2002): 73–105.

Conor, Liz. *The Spectacular Modern Woman: Feminine Visibility in the 1920s*. Bloomington: Indiana University Press, 2004.

de Cordova, Richard. *Picture Personalities: The Emergence of the Star System in America*. Urbana: University of Illinois Press, 1990.

Covarrubias, Miguel. *Mexico South: The Isthmus of Tehuantepec*. New York: A. A. Knopf, 1946.

Craik, Jennifer. *The Face of Fashion: Cultural Studies in Fashion*. London: Routledge, 1994.

Crane, Diana. *Fashion and Its Social Agendas: Class, Gender, and Identity in Clothing*. Chicago: University of Chicago Press, 2000.

Crary, Jonathan. *Techniques of the Observer: On Vision and Modernity in the Nineteenth Century*. Cambridge, Mass: MIT Press, 1990.

Crouch, David, and Nina Lübbren, ed. *Visual Culture and Tourism*. New York: Oxford University Press, 2003.

Cuevas-Wolf, Cristina. "Guillermo Kahlo and Casasola: Architectural Form and Urban Unrest." *History of Photography* 20.3 (1996): 196–207.

Davidson, Caroline. *A Woman's Work Is Never Done: A History of Housework in the British Isles 1650–1950*. London: Chatto and Windus, 1982.

Davidson, Cathy N. "Preface: No More Separate Spheres!" *American Literature* 70.3 (September 1998): 443–63.

Dawson, Alexander. "From Models of the Nation to Model Citizens: Indigenismo and the 'Revindication' of the Mexican Indian, 1920–1940." *Journal of Latin American Studies* 30.2 (May 1998): 279–308.

Debroise, Oliver. *Mexican Suite: A History of Photography in Mexico*, translated and revised in collaboration with Stella de Sá Rego. Austin: University of Texas Press, 2001.

De la Barca, Fanny Calderón. *Life in Mexico during a Residence of Two Years in That Country*. New York: E. P. Dutton, 1931.

Delpar, Helen. *The Enormous Vogue of Things Mexican: Cultural Relations between the United States and Mexico, 1920–1935*. Tuscaloosa: University of Mississippi, 1992.

DeMott, Tom. *Into the Hearts of the Amazons: In Search of a Modern Matriarchy*. Madison, Wisc.: Terrace Books, 2000.

Doane, Mary Ann. "Misrecognition and Identity: The Concept of Identification in Film Theory." In *Plenty to See Everywhere: Explorations in Film Theory*, edited by Ron Burnett. Bloomington: Indiana University Press, 1991.

Douthwaite, Julia V. *Exotic Women: Literary Heroines and Cultural Strategies in Ancien Régime France*. Philadelphia: University of Pennsylvania Press, 1992.

Dussel, Enrique. "Eurocentrism and Modernity." In "Introduction to the Frankfurt Lectures," *Boundary 2* 20.3 (fall 1993): 65–76.

Eckert, Charles. "The Carole Lombard in Macy's Window." In *Fabrications: Costume and the Female Body*, edited by Jane Gaines and Charlotte Herzog. New York: Routledge, 1990.

El turismo norteamericano en México, 1934–1940. Mexico City: Gráfica Panamericana, 1941.

Ewen, Stuart. *Captains of Consciousness: Advertising and the Social Roots of the Consumer Culture*. New York: McGraw-Hill, 1976.

Ewing, Elizabeth. *History of Twentieth Century Fashion*. New York: Charles Scribner's Sons, 1974.

Fallow, Ben. "The Life and Deaths of Felipa Poot: Women, Fiction, and Cardenismo in Postrevolutionary Mexico." *Hispanic American Historical Review* 82.4 (2002): 645–83.

Farnsworth-Alvear, Ann. *Dulcinea in the Factory: Myths, Morals, Men, and Women in Colombia's Industrial Experiment, 1905–1960.* Durham, N.C.: Duke University Press, 2000.

Felski, Rita. *Doing Time: Feminist Theory and Postmodern Culture.* New York: New York University Press, 2000.

——. *The Gender of Modernity.* Cambridge, Mass.: Harvard University Press, 1995.

Fischer, Lucy. *Designing Women: Cinema, Art Deco, and the Female Form.* New York: Columbia University Press, 2003.

Fowler-Salamini, Heather. "Gender, Work, and Coffee in Córdoba, Veracruz, 1850–1910." In *Women of the Mexican Countryside, 1850–1990,* edited by Heather Fowler-Salamini and Mary Kay Vaughan. Tucson: University of Arizona Press, 1994.

——. "Women Coffee Sorters Confront the Mill Owners and the Veracruz Revolutionary State, 1915–1918." *Journal of Women's History* 14.1 (2002): 34–63.

Fowler-Salamini, Heather, and Mary Kay Vaughan. *Women of the Mexican Countryside, 1850–1990.* Tucson: University of Arizona Press, 1994.

Franck, Harry A., and Herbert C. Lanks. *The Pan American Highway: From the Rio Grande to the Canal Zone.* New York: D. Appleton-Century Company, 1942.

Franco, Jean. *Plotting Women: Gender and Representation in Mexico.* New York: Columbia University Press, 1989.

Frederick, Christine. *The New Housekeeping: Efficiency Studies in Home Management.* Garden City, N.Y.: Doubleday, Page and Company, 1916.

Freeman, June. *The Making of the Modern Kitchen: A Cultural History.* Oxford: Berg, 2004.

French, John D., and Daniel James. *The Gendered Worlds of Latin American Women Workers: From Household and Factory to the Union Hall and Ballot Box.* Durham, N.C. Duke University Press, 1997.

French, William. "Imagining and the Cultural History of Nineteenth-century Mexico." *Hispanic American Historical Review* 79:2 (1999): 249–67.

——. *A Peaceful and Working People: Manners, Morals, and Class Formation in Northern Mexico.* Albuquerque: University of New Mexico Press, 1996.

——. "Prostitutes and Guardian Angels: Women, Work, and the Family in Porfirian Mexico." *Hispanic American Historical Review* 72:4 (1992): 529–53.

Friedberg, Anne. "Cinema and the Postmodern Condition." In *Viewing Positions: Ways of Seeing Films,* edited by Linda Williams. New Brunswick, N.J.: Rutgers University Press, 1994.

Frost, Susan Toomey. "Brehme's Picturesque Mexico." Web pages of Susan Toomey Frost. Accessed 10 September 2007. Printouts on file with author.

———. "The Early Maximum Cards of Mexico: Stamps Copied from Real Photo Postcards." Web pages of Susan Toomey Frost. Accessed 10 September 2007. Printouts on file with author.

———. Hugo Brehme's Postcards: A Master Photographer's 20th Century Photo Postcards." Web pages of Susan Toomey Frost. Accessed 10 September 2007. Printouts on file with author.

Gallo, Rubén. *Mexican Modernity: The Avant-Garde and the Technological Revolution*. Cambridge, Mass.: MIT Press, 2005.

Gamboa, Federico. *Santa* (1903). 12th ed. Mexico City: E. Gómez de la Puente, 1927.

Gamio, Manuel. *Forjando patria*. Mexico City: Libreriade Porrúa Hermanos, 1916.

García Calderón, Carola. *Revistas femeninas: La mujer como objeto de consume*. Mexico City: Ediciones El Caballito, 1988.

García Canclini, Néstor. *Consumers and Citizens: Globalization and Multicultural Conflicts*, translated by George Yúdice. Minneapolis: University of Minnesota Press, 2001.

———. *Transforming Modernity: Strategies for Entering and Leaving Modernity*, translated by Christopher L. Chiappari and Silvia L. López. Minneapolis: University of Minnesota Press, 1995.

García Riera, Emilio. *El cine mexicano*. Mexico City: ERA, 1963.

———. Historia del cine mexicano. Mexico City: SEP, 1985.

———. "The Impact of Rancho Grande." In *Mexican Cinema*, edited by Paulo Antonio Paranaguá, translated by Ana López. London: British Film Institute, 1995.

Garvey, Ellen Gruber. *The Adman in the Parlor: Magazines and the Gendering of Consumer Culture, 1880s to 1910s*. New York: Oxford University Press, 1996.

Geary, Christraud M., and Virginia-Lee Webb, eds. *Delivering Views: Distant Cultures in Early Postcards*. Washington, D.C.: Smithsonian Institution Press, 1998.

Giles, Judy. *The Parlour and the Suburb: Domestic Identities, Class, Femininity and Modernity*. Oxford: Berg, 2004.

Gleber, Anke. "Female Flanerie and *The Symphony of the City*." In *Women in the Metropolis: Gender and Modernity in Weimar Culture*, edited by Katharina von ankum. Berkeley: University of California Press, 1997.

Glusker, Susannah Joel. *Anita Brenner: A Mind of Her Own*. Austin: University of Texas Press, 1998.

Goldman, Robert. *Reading Ads Socially*. London: Routledge, 1992.

González, Gilbert G. *Culture of Empire: American Writers, Mexico, and Mexican Immigrants, 1880–1930*. Austin: University of Texas Press, 2004.

González Casanova, Manuel. *Los escritores mexicanos y los inicios delcine, 1896–1907*. Sinaloa: Colegio de Sinaloa, 1995.

Goodspeed, Bernice I. *Mexican Tales: A Compilation of Mexican Stories and Legends*. Mexico City: Editorial Cultura, 1937.

Goolsby, William Berlin. *Guide to Mexico for the Motorist*. Mexico City: by the author, 1936.

Gordon, Sarah A. "'Boundless Possibilities:' Home Sewing and the Meanings of Women's Domestic Work in the United States, 1890–1930." *Journal of Women's History* 16.2 (2004): 68–91.

Graham, Sandra Lauderdale. "Making the Private Public: A Brazilian Perspective." *Journal of Women's History* 15.1 (2003): 28–42.

Graham-Brown, Sarah. *Images of Women: The Portrayal of Women in Photography of the Middle East, 1860–1950*. London: Quartet Books, 1988.

Grazia, Victoria de, with Ellen Furlough, ed. *The Sex of Things: Gender and Consumption in Historical Perspective*. Berkeley: University of California Press, 1996.

———. "The Arts of Purchase: How American Publicity Subverted the European Poster, 1920–1940." In *Remaking History*, edited by Barbara Kruger and Phil Mariani. Seattle: Bay Press, 1989.

Green, Nancy L. *Ready to Wear, Ready to Work: A Century of Industry and Immigrants in Paris and New York*. Durham, N.C.: Duke University Press, 1997.

Green, Venus. "The Impact of Technology upon Women's Work in the Telephone Industry, 1880–1890." PhD diss., Columbia University, New York, 1990.

Grosz, Elizabeth. *Volatile Bodies: Towards a Corporeal Feminism*. Bloomington: Indiana University Press, 1994.

Gruzinski, Serge. *Images at War: Mexico from Columbus to Blade Runner (1942–2019)*, translated by Heather MacLean. Durham, N.C.: Duke University Press, 2001.

Guillén, Mauro F. "Modernism without Modernity: The Rise of Modernist Architecture in Mexico, Brazil, and Argentina, 1890–1940." *Latin American Research Review* 39.2 (2004): 6–34.

Gutiérrez, Natividad. *Nationalist Myths and Ethnic Identities: Indigenous Intellectuals and the Mexican State*. Lincoln: University of Nebraska Press, 1999.

Guy, Donna J. "The Pan American Child Congresses, 1916 to 1942: Pan Americanism, Child Reform, and the Welfare State in Latin America." *Journal of Family History* 23.3 (July 1998): 272–92.

———. "True Womanhood in Latin America." *Journal of Women's History* 14.1 (2002): 170–73.

Haber, Stephen H. *Industry and Underdevelopment: The Industrialization of Mexico, 1890–1940* Stanford: Stanford University Press, 1989.

Hamilton, Nora. *The Limits of State Autonomy: Post-revolutionary Mexico*. Princeton: Princeton University Press, 1982.

Hansen, Roger D. *The Politics of Mexican Development*. Baltimore: Johns Hopkins University Press, 1971.

Hardyment, Christina. *From Mangle to Microwave: The Mechanization of Household Work*. Oxford: Polity Press, 1988.

Harris, Neil. *Cultural Excursions: Marketing Appetites and Cultural Taste in Modern America*. Chicago: University of Chicago Press, 1990.

Harvey, David. *The Condition of Postmodernity: An Enquiry into the Origins of Cultural Change*. Cambridge, Mass.: Oxford University Press, 1990.

Herrera, Hayden. *Frida: Biography of Frida Kahlo*. New York: Harper and Row, 1983.

Hershfield, Joanne. *Mexican Cinema/Mexican Woman: 1940–1950*. Tucson: University of Arizona Press, 1996.

Herzog, Charlotte Cornelia, and Jane Marie Gaines. "Puffed Sleeves before Tea-Time." In *Stardom Industry of Desire*, edited by Christine Gledhill. London: Routledge: 1991.

Heyman, Josiah McC. "Imports and Standards of Justice on the Mexico-United States Border." In *The Allure of the Foreign: Imported Goods in Postcolonial Latin America*. Ann Arbor: University of Michigan Press, 1997.

Hill, Daniel Delis. *Advertising to the American Woman, 1900–1999*. Columbus: Ohio State University Press, 2002.

Hollander, Ann. *Moving Pictures*. New York: Alfred A. Knopf, 1989.

———. *Seeing through Clothes*. New York: Viking Press, 1978.

Horowitz, Daniel. *The Morality of Spending: Attitudes toward the Consumer Society in America, 1875–1940*. Baltimore: Johns Hopkins University Press, 1985.

Howes, David, ed. *Cross-Cultural Consumption: Global Markets, Local Realities*. London: Routledge, 1996.

———. "Introduction: Commodities and Cultural Borders." In *Cross-Cultural Consumption*.

Hoy, Suellen. *Chasing Dirt: The American Pursuit of Cleanliness*. New York: Oxford University Press, 1995.

Huneault, Kristina. *Difficult Subjects: Working Women and Visual Culture, Britain 1880–1914*. Aldershot: Ashgate, 2002.

Jobling, Paul. *Fashion Spreads: Word and Image in Fashion Photography since 1980*. Oxford: Berg, 1999.

Jones, Jennifer M. "Repackaging Rousseau: Femininity and Fashion in Old Regime France." *French Historical Studies* 18.4 (fall 1994): 940–76.

Joseph, Gilbert M., and Daniel Nugent, ed. *Everyday Forms of State Formation: Revolution and the Negotiation of Rule in Modern Mexico*. Durham, N.C.: Duke University Press, 1994.

Joseph, Gilbert M., Anne Rubenstein, and Eric Zolov, eds. *Fragments of a Golden Age: The Politics of Culture in Mexico since 1940*. Durham, N.C.: Duke University Press, 2001.

Kapelusz-Poppi, Ana María. "Rural Health and State Construction in Post-revolutionary Mexico: The Nicolaita Project for Rural Medical Services." *Americas* 58.2 (2001): 261–83.

Kaplan, Amy. "Manifest Domesticity." *American Literature*, 70.3 (1998): 581–606.

Katz, Michael B., Mark J. Stern, and Jamie J. Fader. "Women and the Paradox of Economic Inequality in the Twentieth-Century." *Journal of Social History* 39.1 (2005):65–88.

Keep, Christopher. "The Cultural Work of the Type-Writer Girl." *Victorian Studies* 40.3 (1997): 401–26.

Kimmel, Michael. "Introduction: The Power of Gender and the Gender of Power." In *The Material Culture of Gender, The Gender of Material Culture*, edited by Katharine Martinez and Kenneth L. Ames. Winterthur, Del.: Henry Francis du Pont Winterthur Museum, 1997.

King, Timothy. *Mexico: Industrialization and Trade Policies since 1940*. London: Oxford University Press, 1970.

Kitch, Carolyn. *The Girl on the Magazine Cover: The Origins of Visual Stereotypes in American Mass Media*. Chapel Hill: The University of North Carolina Press, 2001.

Kluger, Richard. *Ashes to Ashes: America's Hundred-Year Cigarette War, the Publish Health, and the Unabashed Triumph of Philip Morris*. New York: Vintage Books, 1997.

Knight, Alan. "Cardenismo: Juggernaut or Jalopy?" *Journal of Latin American Studies* 26.2 (1994): 73–107.

———. "Popular Culture and the Revolutionary State in Mexico, 1910–1940." *The Hispanic American Historical Review* 74.3 (1994): 393–444.

———. "Revolutionary Project, Recalcitrant People: Mexico, 1910–40." In *The Revolutionary Process in Mexico: Essays on Political and Social Change, 1880–1940*, edited by Jaime E. Rodríguez O. Los Angeles: UCLA Latin American Center Publications, 1990.

———. "The Working Class and the Mexican Revolution." *Journal of Latin American Studies* 16 (May 1984): 51–97.

Köhler, Angelika. *Ambivalent Desires: The New Woman between Social Modernization and Modern Writing*. Heidelberg: Universitätsverlag WINTER, 2004.

Kozol, Wendy. *Life's America: Family and Nation in Postwar Photojournalism*. Philadelphia: Temple University Press, 1994.

Kwolek-Folland, Angel. "The Gendered Environment of the Corporate Workplace, 1880–1930." In *The Material Culture of Gender, The Gender of Material Culture*, edited by Katharine Martinez and Kenneth L. Ames. Winterthur, Del.: Henry Francis du Pont Winterthur Museum, 1997.

Landes, Joan B. *Visualizing the Nation: Gender, Representation, and Revolution in Eighteenth-Century France*. Ithaca: Cornell University Press, 2001.

Larraín, Jorge. *Identity and Modernity in Latin America*. Cambridge: Polity Press, 2000.

Laver, James. *Costume and Fashion: A Concise History*. New York: Oxford University Press, 1983.

Lavin, Maud. "Photomontage, Mass Culture, and Modernity: Utopianism in the Circle of New Advertising Designers." In *Montage and Modern Life, 1919–1942*, edited by Matthew Teitelbaum. Cambridge, Mass.: MIT Press, 1992.

Lear, John. *Workers, Neighbors, and Citizens: The Revolution in Mexico City*. Lincoln: University of Nebraska Press, 2001.

Lears, T. Jackson. *Fables of Abundance: A Cultural History of Advertising in America*. New York: Basic Books, 1994.

———. "Uneasy Courtship: Modern Art and Modern Advertising." *American Quarterly* 39.1 (spring 1987): 133–54.

Leavitt, Sarah A. *From Catharine Beecher to Martha Stewart: A Cultural History of Domestic Advice*. Chapel Hill: University of North Carolina Press, 2002.

Lefebvre, Henri H. *The Production of Space*, translated by Donald Nicholson-Smith. Oxford: Blackwell, 1991.

———. *Everyday Life in the Modern World*, translated by Sacha Rabinovitch. New Brunswick, N.J.: Transaction Publishers, 1984.

Leiss, William, Stephen Kline, and Sut Jhally. *Social Communication in Advertising: Persons, Products, and Images of Well-Being*. New York: Methuen, 1986.

Leonardo, Micaela di. *Exotics at Home: Anthropologies, Others, American Modernity*. Chicago: University of Chicago Press, 1998.

Lewis, Oscar. *Tepoztlán: Village in Mexico*. New York: Henry Holt and Company, 1960.

Lipartito, Kenneth. "When Women Were Switches: Technology, Work, and Gender in the Telephone Industry, 1890–1920." *American Historical Review* 99.4 (October 1994): 1075–11.

Lipovetsky, Gilles. *The Empire of Fashion: Dressing Modern Democracy*, translated by Catherine Porter. Princeton: Princeton University Press, 1994.

Lomnitz-Adler, Claudio. *Deep Mexico, Silent Mexico: An Anthropology of Nationalism*. Minneapolis: University of Minnesota Press, 2001.

——. *Exits from the Labyrinth: Culture and Ideology in the Mexican National Space*. Berkeley: University of California Press, 1992.

López, Ana M. "Early Cinema and Modernity in Latin America." *Cinema Journal* 40.1 (fall 2000): 47–78.

López, Rick A. "The India Bonita Context of 1921 and the Ethnicization of Mexican National Culture." *Hispanic American Historical Review* 8:22 (2002): 291–328.

——. "Lo Más Mexicano de México: Popular Arts, Indians, and Urban Intellectuals in the Ethnicization of Postrevolutionary National Culture, 1920–1972." PhD diss., Yale University, New Haven, 2001.

Marchand, Roland. *Advertising the American Dream: Making Way for Modernity, 1920–1930*. Berkeley: University of California Press, 1985.

Marcus, Sharon. "Reflections on Victorian Fashion Plates." In *differences: A Journal of Feminist Cultural Studies* 14.3 (2003): 4–33.

Margueritte, Victor. *La garçonne*, Paris: E. Flammarion, 1922.

Martín-Barbero, Jesús. *Communication, Culture, and Hegemony: From the Media to Mediations*, translated by Elizabeth Fox and Robert A. White. London: Sage, 1992.

Marvin, Carolyn. *When Old technologies Were New: Thinking about Electric Communication in the Late Nineteenth Century*. New York: Oxford University Press, 1988.

Mason, Peter. *Infelicities: Representations of the Exotic*. Baltimore: Johns Hopkins University Press, 1998.

Matthews, Glenna. *"Just a Housewife": The Rise and Fall of Domesticity in America*. New York: Oxford University Press, 1987.

McClintock, Anne. *Imperial Leather: Race, Gender, and Sexuality in the Colonial Contest*. New York: Routledge, 1995.

McHugh, Kathleen Anne. *American Domesticity: From How-to Manual to Hollywood Melodrama*. New York: Oxford University Press, 1999.

Meikle, Jeffrey L. "Domesticating Modernity: Ambivalence and Appropriation, 1920–1940." In *Designing Modernity: The Arts of Reform and Persuasion, 1885–1945*, edited by Wendy Kaplan. New York: Thames and Hudson, 1995.

Mejia Barquera, Fernando. *La industria de la radio y la televisión y la política del estado mexicano (1920–1960)*. Mexico City: Fundación Manuel Buendia, 1989.

Meléndez, Mariselle. "Visualizing Difference: The Rhetoric of Clothing in Colonial Spanish America." In *The Latin American Fashion Reader*, edited by Regina A. Root Oxford: Berg, 2005.

Mendes, Valerie, and Amy de la Haye. *20th Century Fashion*. London: Thames and Hudson, 1999.

Meyer, Susan E. *America's Great Illustrators*. New York: H. N. Abrams, 1978.

Meyers, Charles Nash. *Education and National Development in Mexico*. Princeton: Industrial Relations Section, Department of Economics, Princeton University, 1965.

Mexican National Railroad. *Tropical Tours to Toltec Towns in Mexico*. Chicago: Rogers and Smith Company, 1898.

Miller, Heather Lee. "Trick Identities: The Nexus of Work and Sex." *Journal of Women's History* 15.4 (2004): 145–52.

Mirzoeff, Nicholas. *An Introduction to Visual Culture*. New York: Routledge, 1999.

Mitchell, W. J. T. *Picture Theory*. Chicago: University of Chicago Press, 1994.

Monsiváis, Carlos. "Mythologies." In *Mexican Cinema*, edited by Paulo Antonio Paranaguá, translated by Ana M. López. London: British Film Institute, 1995.

Monsiváis, Carlos, and Carlos Bonfil. *A través del espejo: El cine Mexicano y su público*. Mexico City: Ediciones el Milagro, 1994.

Montellano, Francisco. *Charles B. Waite: La época de oro de las postales en México*. Mexico City: Consejo Nacional para la Cultura y las Artes, 1998.

Moreno, Julio. "J. Walter Thompson, the Good Neighbor Policy, and Lessons in Mexican Business Culture, 1920–1950." *Enterprise and Society* 5.2 (2004): 254–80.

———. *Yankee Don't Go Home! Mexican Nationalism, American Business Culture, and the Shaping of Modern Mexico, 1920–1950*. Chapel Hill: University of North Carolina Press, 2003.

Mraz, John "Envisioning Mexico: Photography and National Identity." Working Paper 32, Duke–University of North Carolina Program in Latin American Studies, Durham, N.C., 2001.

———. "Picturing Mexico's Past: Photography and *Historia Gráfica*." *South Central Review* 21.3 (2004): 24–45.

———. "From Positivism to Populism: Toward a History of Photojournalism in Mexico." *Afterimage* 18.5 (January 1991).

———. "'Today, Tomorrow, and Always': The Golden Age of Illustrated Magazines in Mexico, 1937–1960." In *Fragments of a Golden Age: The Politics of Culture in Mexico since 1940*, edited by Joseph, Gilbert M., Anne Rubenstein, and Eric Zolov. Durham, N.C.: Duke University Press, 2001.

Muñoz, Elsa. *Cuerpo, representación y poder: México en los albores de la reconstrucción, 1920–1934*. Mexico City: Universidad Autónoma Metropolitana, 2002.

Murphy, D. "Mexican Tourism, 1876–1940: The Socio-economic, Political, and Infrastructural Effects of a Developing Leisure Industry." MA Thesis, Department of History, University of North Carolina, Chapel Hill, 1988.

Newcomer, Daniel. *Reconciling Modernity: Urban State Formation in 1940s León, Mexico*. Lincoln: University of Nebraska Press, 2004.

Nickles, Shelley. "Preserving Women: Refrigerator Design as Social Process in the 1930s." *Technology and Culture* 43.4 (2002): 693–727.

Noble, Andrea. "Photography and Vision in Porfirian Mexico." *Cultura Visual en América Latina* 9.1 (January–June 1998).

Norris, James D. *Advertising and the Transformation of American Society, 1865–1920.* New York: Greenwood Press, 1990.

O'Gorman, Edmundo. *Destierro de sombras: Luz en el origen de la imagen y culto de Nuestra Señora de Guadalupe del Tepeyac.* Mexico City: Universidad Nacional Autónoma de México, 1986.

O'Keefe, A. M., and R. W. Pollay. "Deadly Targeting of Women in Promoting Cigarettes." *Journal of the American Medical Women's Association* 51.1 and 51.2 (1996): 67–69.

Olcott, Jocelyn. *Revolutionary Women in Postrevolutionary Mexico.* Durham, N.C.: Duke University Press, 2005.

———. "'Worthy Wives and Mothers': State-Sponsored Women's Organizing in Post-revolutionary Mexico." *Journal of Women's History* 13.4 (winter 2002): 106–31.

O'Malley, Ilene V. *The Myth of the Mexican Revolution: Hero Cults and the Institutionalization of the Mexican State, 1920–1940.* New York: Greenwood Press, 1986.

Palmer, Phyllis. *Domesticity and Dirt: Housewives and Domestic Servants in the United States, 1920–1935.* Philadelphia, Temple University Press, 1989.

Pattison, Mary. *The Principles of Domestic Management.* New York: Trow Press, 1915.

Paulicelli, Eugenia. *Fashion under Fascism.* Oxford: Berg, 2004.

Peiss, Cathy. *Cheap Amusements: Working Women and Leisure in Turn-of-the-Century New York.* Philadelphia: Temple University Press, 1985.

———. *Hope in a Jar: The Making of America's Beauty Culture.* New York: Henry Holt and Company, 1998.

———. "Making up, Making over: Cosmetics, Consumer Culture, and Women's Identity." In *The Sex of Things: Gender and Consumption in Historical Perspective*, edited by de Grazia with Ellen Furlough. Berkeley: University of California Press, 1996.

Penyak, Lee M. "Obstetrics and the Emergence of Women in Mexico's Medical Establishment." *Americas* 60.1 (2003): 59–85.

Pérez Montfort, Ricardo. "Contrapunto de la imagen nacionalista: El estereotipo norteamericano en el cine de charros 1920–1946." In *México-Estados Unidos: Encuentros y desencuentros en el cine*, edited by Ignacio Durán, Iván Trujillo, and Mónica Verea. Mexico City: Universidad Nacional Autónoma de México, 1996.

———. "Indigenismo, hispanismo y panamericanismo en la cultura popular mexicana de 1920 a 1940." In *Cultura e identidad nacional*, edited by Roberto Blancarte. Mexico City: Consejo Nacional para la Cultura y las Artes, 1994.

Peterson, Jeanette Favrot. "Creating the Virgin of Guadalupe: The Cloth, the Artist, the Sources, in Sixteenth-Century New Spain." *The Americas* 61.4 (April 2005): 571–610.

Piccato, Pablo. *City of Suspects: Crime in Mexico City, 1900–1930*. Durham, N.C.: Duke University Press, 2001.

Piepmeier, Alison. *Out in Public: Configurations of Women's Bodies in Nineteenth-Century America*. Chapel Hill: University of North Carolina Press, 2004.

Pilcher, Jeffrey M. *¡Que Vivan los Tamales! Food and the Making of Mexican Identity*. Diálogos Series. Albuquerque: University of New Mexico Press, 1998.

Pollock, Griselda. *Vision and Difference: Femininity, Feminism, and Histories of Art*. London: Routledge, 1988.

Poole, Deborah. "An Image of "Our Indian": Type Photographs and Racial Sentiments in Oaxaca, 1920–1940." *Hispanic American Historical Review* 84.1 (February 2004): 37–82.

———. *Vision, Race, and Modernity: A Visual Economy of the Andean Image World*. Princeton: Princeton University Press, 1997.

Porter, Susie S. "'And That It Is Custom Makes It Law': Class Conflict and Gender Ideology in the Public Sphere, Mexico City, 1880–1910." *Social Science History* 24.1 (spring 2000): 111–48.

———. *Working Women in Mexico City: Public Discourses and Material Conditions, 1879–1931*. Tucson: University of Arizona Press, 2003.

Potter, David. *People of Plenty: Economic Abundance and the American Character*. Chicago: University of Chicago Press, 1958.

Raat, W. Dirk. *Mexico and the United States: Ambivalent Vistas*. 3rd ed. Athens: University of Georgia Press, 2004.

Radway, Janice. *Reading the Romance: Women, Patriarchy and Popular Literature*. Chapel Hill: University of North Carolina Press, 1984.

Ramos Escandón, Carmen. *Presencia y Transparencia: la mujer en la historia de México*. Mexico City: El Colegio de México, 1987.

Randall, Kimberly. "The Traveler's Eye: Chinas Poblanas and European-Inspired Costume in Postcolonial Mexico." In *The Latin American Fashion Reader*, edited by Regina A. Root. Oxford: Berg, 2005.

Redfield, Robert. *Tepoztlan, a Mexican Village: A Study of Folk Life*. Chicago: University of Illinois Press, 1930.

Reyes, Aurelio de los. *Medio siglo de cine Mexicano (1896–1947)*. Mexico City: Editorial Trillas, 1987.

Rivera-Garza, Cristina. "The Criminalization of the Syphilitic Body: Prostitutes,

Health Crimes, and Society in Mexico City, 1867–1930." In *Crime and Punishment in Latin America: Law and Society since Late Colonial Times*, edited by Ricardo D. Salvatore, Carlos Aguirre, and Gilbert Joseph. Durham, N.C.: Duke University Press, 2001.

Roberts, Mary Louise. *Civilization without Sexes: Reconstructing Gender in Postwar France, 1917–1927*. Chicago: University of Chicago Press, 1994.

———. "Samson and Delilah Revisited: The Politics of Women's Fashion in 1920s France." *American Historical Review* 98.3 (June 1993): 657–84.

Root, Regina A., ed. *The Latin American Fashion Reader*. Oxford: Berg, 2005.

Rosenberger, Nancy R. "Fragile Resistance, Signs of Status: Women between State and Media in Japan." In *Re-imaging Japanese Women*, edited by Anne E. Imamura. Berkeley: University of California Press, 1996.

Rotella, Elyse J. "The Transformation of the American Office: Changes in Employment and Technology." *Journal of Economic History* 41.1 (March 1981): 51–57.

Rowe, William, and Vivian Schelling. *Memory and Modernity: Popular Culture in Latin America*. London: Verso, 1991.

Rubenstein, Anne. *Bad Language, Naked Ladies, and Other Threats to the Nation: A Political History of Comic Books in Mexico*. Durham, N.C.: Duke University Press, 1998.

Rydell, Robert W. "Souvenirs of Imperialism: World's Fair Postcards." In *Delivering Views: Distant Cultures in Early Postcards*, edited by Christraud M. Geary and Virginia-Lee Webb. Washington, D.C.: Smithsonian Institution Press, 1998.

Sagredo, Rafael. *"María Villa (a) La Chiquita no. 4002."* Mexico City: Cal y Arena, 1996.

Santaolalla, Isabel. "Introduction." 2000a. In *"New" Exoticisms: Changing Patterns in the Construction of Otherness*.

Santaolalla, Isabel, ed. *"New" Exoticisms: Changing Patterns in the Construction of Otherness*. Atlanta: Rodopi, 2000b.

Saragoza, Alex. "The Selling of Mexico: Tourism and the State, 1929–1952." In *Fragments of a Golden Age: The Politics of Culture in Mexico since 1940*, edited by Gilbert M. Joseph, Anne Rubenstein, and Eric Zolov. Durham, N.C.: Duke University Press, 2001.

Sayer, Chloë. *Costumes of Mexico*. Austin: University of Texas Press, 1985.

Scanlon, Jennifer. *Inarticulate Longings: The Ladies' Home Journal, Gender, and the Promises of Consumer Culture*. London: Routledge, 1995.

Schell, Patience A. "Nationalizing Children through Schools and Hygiene: Porfirian and Revolutionary Mexico City." *Americas* 60.4 (2004): 559–87.

———. "Teaching the Children of the Revolution: Church and State Education in Mexico City, 1917–1926." PhD diss., St. Antony's College, Oxford University, 1998.

Schmidt, Henry C. *The Roots of Lo Mexicano: Self and Society in Mexican Thought, 1900–1934*. College Station: Texas A&M University, 1978.

Schwartz Cowan, Ruth. *More Work for Mother: The Ironies of Household Technology from the Open Hearth to the Microwave*. New York: Basic Books, 1983.

Scott, Joan. *Feminism and History*. New York: Oxford University Press, 1996.

Segrave, Kerry. *Women and Smoking in America, 1880–1950*. Jefferson, N.C.: McFarland and Company, 2005.

Sekula, Allan. "The Body in the Archive." *October* 39 (winter 1986): 3–64.

——. *Photography against the Grain*. Halifax: Press of Nova Scotia College of Art and Design, 1984.

Semmerling, Tim Jon. *Israeli and Palestinian Postcards: Presentations of National Self*. Austin: University of Texas Press, 2004.

Shevelow, Kathryn. *Women and Print Culture: The Construction of Femininity in the Early Periodical*. London: Routledge, 1989.

Shuttleworth, Sally. "Female Circulation: Medical Discourse and Popular Advertising in the Mid-Victorian Era." In *Body/Politics*, edited by M. Jacobus. London: Routledge, 1990.

Sigel, Lisa Z. "Filth in the Wrong People's Hands: Postcards and the Expansion of Pornography in Britain and the Atlantic World, 1880–1917." *Journal of Social History* 33.4 (2000): 859–85.

Silverstone, Richard, Eric Hirsch, and David Morley. "Information and Communication Technologies and the Moral Economy of the Household." In *Consuming Technologies. Media and Information in Domestic Spaces*, edited by R. Silverstone and Eric Hirch. London: Routledge, 2003.

Sivulka, Juliann. *Soap, Sex, and Cigarettes: A Cultural History of American Advertising*. Belmont, Calif.: Wadsworth Publishing Company, 1998.

——. *Stronger Than Dirt: A Cultural History of Advertising Personal Hygiene in America, 1875 to 1940*. Amherst, N.Y.: Humanity Books, 2001.

Smith, Robert F. *The United States and Revolutionary Nationalism in Mexico, 1916–1932*. Chicago: University of Chicago Press, 1972.

Smith-Rosenberg, Carroll. "Political Camp or the Ambiguous Engendering of the American Republic." In *Gendered Nations: Nationalisms and Gender Order the Long Nineteenth Century*, edited by Ida Blom, Karen Hagemann, and Catherine Hall. Oxford: Berg, 2000.

Snodgrass, Michael. *Deference and Defiance in Monterrey: Workers, Paternalism, and Revolution in Mexico, 1890–1950*. Cambridge: Cambridge University Press, 2003.

Sontag, Susan. *On Photography*. Harmondsworth: Penguin, 1979.

Soto, Shirlene Ann. *The Mexican Woman: A Study of Her Participation in the Revolution, 1910–1940*. Palo Alto: R & E Research Associates, 1979.

Sparke, Penny. *An Introduction to Design and Culture in the Twentieth Century*. New York: Harper and Row, 1987.

Stacey, Jackie. *Star-gazing: Hollywood Cinema and Female Spectatorship*. London: Routledge, 1994.

Staff, Frank. *The Picture Postcard and Its Origins*. New York: Frederick A. Praeger, 1966.

Steele, Valerie. *Paris Fashion: A Cultural History*. New York: Oxford University Press, 1988.

Stein, Sally. "'Good Fences Make Good Neighbors': American Resistance to Photomontage between the Wars." In *Montage and Modern Life, 1919–1942*, edited by Matthew Teitelbaum. Cambridge, Mass.: MIT Press, 1992.

Stepan, Nancy Leys. *The Hour of Eugenics*. Ithaca: Cornell University Press, 1991.

Stern, Alexandra Minna. "Responsible Mothers and Normal Children: Eugenics, Nationalism, and Welfare in Post-revolutionary Mexico, 1920–1940." *Journal of Historical Sociology* 12.4 (December 1999): 369–97.

Stern, Steve J. *The Secret History of Gender: Women, Men, and Power in Late Colonial Mexico*. Chapel Hill: University of North Carolina Press, 1995.

Stevens, Evelyn P. "Marianismo: The Other Face of Machismo." In *Confronting Change, Challenging Tradition: Women in Latin American History*, edited by Gertrude M. Yeager. Wilmington, Del.: SR Books, 1994.

Stevens, Sarah E. "Figuring Modernity: The New Woman and the Modern Girl in Republican China." *NWSA Journal* 15.3 (2003): 82–103.

Stewart, Mary Lynn. *For Health and Beauty: Physical Culture for Frenchwomen, 1880s–1930s*. Baltimore: John Hopkins University Press, 2001.

Story, Dale. *Industry, the State, and Public Policy in Mexico*. Austin: University of Texas Press, 1986.

Strom, Sharon Hartman. "'Light Manufacturing': The Feminization of American Office Work, 1900–1930." *Industrial and Labor Relations Review* 43.1 (October 1989): 53–71.

Tagg, John. *The Burden of Representation*. Minneapolis: University of Minnesota Press, 1993.

——. "Evidence, Truth and Order: Photographic Records and the Growth of the State." *Ten8*, no. 13 (1984): 10–12.

Tenorio-Trillo, Mauricio. *Mexico at the World's Fairs: Crafting a Modern Nation*. Berkeley: University of California Press, 1996.

Terry, T. Philip. *Terry's Guide to Mexico*. Boston: Houghton Mifflin, 1929.

Thiesse, Ann-Marie. "Democracy Softens Force of Change: Inventing National

Identity." Le Monde Diplomatique, Global Policy Forum, 1999. Web pages of Global Policy Forum, accessed 12 September 2007. Printouts on file with author.

Tiersten, Lisa. *Marianne in the Market: Envisioning Consumer Society in Fin-de-Siècle France*. Berkeley: University of California Press, 2001.

Tilly, Louise A. "Industrialization and Gender Inequality." Working Paper 148, Center for Studies of Social Change, New York, 1992.

Tilly, Louise A., and Joan Scott. *Women, Work, and Family*. New York: Holt, Rinehart and Winston, 1978.

Tobey, Ronald C. *Technology as Freedom: The New Deal and the Electrical Modernization of the American Home*. Berkeley: University of California Press, 1996.

Torres, Luis R., and María del Carmen Ruiz Casteñeda. *El periodismo en México: 500 años de historia*. Mexico City: Edamex, 1995.

Towner, Margaret. "Monopoly Capitalism and Women's Work During the Porfiriato." *Latin American Perspectives* 4.1/2 (winter 1977): 90–105.

Tuñón Pablos, Julia. *Women in Mexico: A Past Unveiled*, translated by Alan Hynds. Austin: University of Texas Press, 1999.

Turner, Frederick. "Los efectos de la participación femenina en la Revolución de 1910." *Historial Mexicana* 16.4 (April–June 1991): 603–20.

Urry, John. *The Tourist Gaze*. 2nd ed. London: Sage Publications, 2002.

Vallens, Vivian M. *Working Women in Mexico during the Porfiriato, 1880–1990*. San Francisco: R and E Research Associates, 1978.

Vanderwood, Paul J. *Border Fury: A Picture-Postcard Record of Mexico's Revolution and U.S. War Preparedness, 1910–1919*. Albuquerque: University of New Mexico Press, 1988.

Vasconcelos, José. *La raza cósmica: misión de la raza iberoamericana*. Paris: Agencia Mundial de Librería, 1982.

Vasconcelos, José, and Manuel Gamio. *Aspects of Mexican Civilization: Lectures on the Harris Foundation 1926*. Chicago: University of Chicago Press, 1926.

Vaughan, Mary Kay. *Cultural Politics in Revolution: Teachers, Peasants, and Schools in Mexico, 1930–1940*. Tucson: University of Arizona Press, 1997.

———. "Modernizing Patriarchy: State Policies, Rural Households, and Women in Mexico, 1930–1940." In *Hidden Histories of Gender and the State in Latin American*, edited by Elizabeth Dore and Maxine Molyreux. Durham, N.C.: Duke University Press, 2000.

———. "Rural Women's Literacy and Education during the Mexican Revolution: *Subverting a Patriarchal Event?*" In *Women of the Mexican Countryside, 1850–1990*, edited by Heather Fowler-Salamini and Mary Kay Vaughan. Tucson: University of Arizona Press, 1994.

Vaughan, Mary Kay, and Stephen E. Lewis. *The Eagle and the Virgin: Nation and*

Cultural Revolution in Mexico, 1920–1940. Durham, N.C.: Duke University Press, 2006.

Vázquez, Josefina. "La sociedad mexicana en la primera mitad del siglo XIX." In *Antología de textos, cultura mexicana*, edited by María Carmen Elizundía Ponce. Mexico City: Universidad Anáhuac del Sur, 1999.

Vega Alfaro, Eduardo de la. "Origins, Development and Crisis of the Sound Cinema (1929–64)." In *Mexican Cinema*, edited by Paulo Antonio Paranaguá. London: British Film Institute, 1995.

Vinikas, Vincent. *Soft Soap, Hard Sell: American Hygiene in an Age of Advertisement*. Ames: Iowa State University Press, 1992.

Virilio, Paul. *The Vision Machine*. Bloomington: Indiana University Press, 1994.

Walby, Sylvia. "Woman and Nation." In *Mapping the Nation*, edited by Gopal Balakrishnan. London: Verso, 1996.

Walker, John A., and Sarah Chaplin. *Visual Culture: An Introduction*. Manchester: Manchester University Press, 1997.

Walkowitz, Judith. *Prostitution and Victorian Society: Women, Class, and the State*. Cambridge: Cambridge University Press, 1982.

Wang, Ning. *Tourism and Modernity: A Sociological Analysis*. Amsterdam: Pergamon, 2000.

Ward, Jane. *Weimar Surfaces: Urban Visual Culture in 1920s Germany*. Berkeley: University of California Press, 2001.

Wells, David R. *Consumerism and the Movement of Housewives into Wage Work: The Interaction of Patriarchy, Class and Capitalism in Twentieth Century America*. Singapore: Ashgate Publishing, 1998.

Welter, Barbara. "The Cult of True Womanhood, 1820–1860." *American Quarterly* 18 (1966): 151–74.

White, Cynthia L. *Women's Magazines, 1693–1968*. London: Michael Joseph Books, 1970.

Wilson, Elizabeth. *Adorned in Dreams: Fashion and Modernity*. Berkeley: University of California Press, 1987.

———. *The Sphinx in the City: Urban Life, the Control of Disorder, and Women*. Berkeley: University of California Press, 1992.

Wolff, Janet. *Feminine Sentences: Essays on Women and Culture*. Berkeley: University of California Press, 1990.

Wolkowitz, Carol. "The Working Body as Sign: Historical Snapshots." In *Constructing Gendered Bodies*, edited by Kathryn Backett-Milburn and Linda McKie. Hampshire: Palgrave Macmillan, 2001.

Woodard, James P. "Marketing Modernity: The J. Walter Thompson Company and North American Advertising in Brazil, 1929–1939." *Hispanic American Historical Review* 8:22 (2002): 257–90.

Woody, Howard. "International Postcards: Their History, Production, and Distribution (Circa 1895–1915)." In *Delivering Views: Distant Cultures in Early Postcards*, edited by Christraud M. Geary and Virginia-Lee Webb. Washington, D.C.: Smithsonian Institution Press, 1998.

Wosk, Julie. *Women and the Machine: Representations from the Spinning Wheel to the Electronic Age*. Baltimore: Johns Hopkins University Press, 2001.

Yuval-Davis, Nira. *Gender and Nation*. London: Sage, 1997.

Index